DOWN TO EARTH

TERRESTRIAL ACTIVITIES

The Collected Works
of Gregge Tiffen

P Systems & Associates, Publishers
La Jolla, California

Copyright 2010
By
G-Systems International

All Rights Reserved

ISBN: 978-0-9842552-4-5

P Systems & Associates, Publishers
La Jolla, California

Down to Earth: Terrestrial Activities
Published by P Systems & Associates
P.O. Box 12754
La Jolla, CA 92039
www.P-SystemsInc.com

While we appreciate your enthusiasm for sharing our work, please remind yourself of what you know about copyrighted information. Here's a refresher: All rights Reserved. No parts of this publication may be reproduced, stored in or introduced into a retrieval system, or transmitted, in any form or by any means (electronic, mechanical, photocopying, recording or otherwise), without the prior written consent. The scanning, uploading, and distribution of this book via the Internet or by any other means without the permission of G-Systems International is illegal and punishable by law. Your support of these rights is appreciated. Thank you.

To contact G-Systems International, visit www.g-systems.com, email Bonnie@g-systems.com, or call 1-972-447-9092.

For general information about other publications, visit our web site www.P-SystemsInc.com or call our toll free number 1.888.658.0668.

Transcribed and written by Patrece Powers
Graphic Design: Isla Cordelae
Editorial assistance: Cindy Reinhardt
                      Isla Cordelae
                      Renne Evans

Printed in the United States of America
on recycled paper (80% post consumer)

In honor of Mother Nature

She offers all terrestrials the abundant
and necessary conditions to receive
real and tangible experiences.

These Works of mysticism update that which would otherwise be left behind.

--Gregge Tiffen

Contents

Introduction: The Collected Works 1

The Subterranean Society 3
   1. The Earth Plane 6
   2. Adjustment Period 9
   3. Single Functioning Unit 11
   4. Population. 13
   5. Physical Features 14
   6. Aging Indicators. 16
   7. Atmosphere. 16
   8. Socialization 17
   9. Astral Visits. 18
  10. One Step Up 20

Alien Territory. 21
   1. Life Force. 21
   2. Earth Body. 25
   3. Interior Alien. 27
   4. The Will to Survive 33
   5. Conformity 34
   6. Nature's Law. 36
   7. Nature's Action 38
   8. The Law of Cause and Effect 40
   9. Nature's Needs. 41
  10. The Natural Key to Life. 41
  11. Empowerment 43

Family Ties. 45
   1. Well Positioned. 47
   2. Genetic Seeds 49
   3. In Control 52
   4. By Design. 54
   5. Humanoids 56
   6. A State of Refinement 59

Conclusion: Terrestrial Activities 61
  1. You Are Here 66
  2. Direction 67
  3. Elements of Interference 69
  4. Social Security 76
  5. Magnetic Attraction 77
  6. Getting the Most Out of Life 82
  7. Investments 84
  8. What's the Point? 86
  9. Habit Training 87
 10. Down to Earth 91

Appendix 93

Introduction
The Collected Works

The Collected Works is a compilation of presentations from Gregge Tiffen's lectures and teachings to which the reader can return beneficially time and time again. Gregge had little time to write due to the sheer magnitude of teaching and lecturing activities that increased year-by-year throughout more than five decades of his work in the field of meta-energy. In addition to his business consultations and lectures, his days were spent meeting the needs of people who sought guidance for personal and professional concerns.

He consistently refused requests to form an organization of any kind in order to insure that his unique training in mysticism, including the Universal Laws of Independence and Individuality, would find the proper audience. He felt certain that such teachings must not be frame-worked within organizations. By their very design, organizations develop a hierarchy of personalities that regrettably destroy the atmosphere necessary for the purity required to learn and to teach, to lead and to follow.

The style and presentation of materials published in this series of The Collected Works are Gregge's unaltered spoken words. There is very little editorial license in order to maintain the clarity of precision that identifies how he was taught and, as a result, how he taught. The timeless nature of knowledge precludes indicating dates and locations of his teachings. In this way, we are able to support and promote the integrity of Gregge's life-long dedication to up-date and correct misinterpretations of ancient wisdoms.

Since all lectures were delivered to an audience familiar with Gregge's mystical training and orientation, we suggest those who are unacquainted with those principles familiarize themselves by reading his highly acclaimed book: *Life in the World Hereafter, The Journey Continues.* It is truly an adventure you won't want to miss. Don't leave earth without it!

Part I
The Subterranean Society

> *Survival is the energy*
> *that humanly motivates us.*
> *--GT*

I am going to go into the area of the technicalities, as it were, of the occult aspects in the Universe. When we get involved in the consideration of metaphysics, we often consider planets out in the Universe where there is no edge. It is the enormity that has to be met before we can even talk about a single planet because it is in the immensity that we find the seeds. There isn't a telescope yet that has explored the vast enormity of the Universe.

Every astral body and every planet that we have in the Universe has a distinctive function. Its function as far as you are concerned is one of a classroom function. Any place that you can go in the Universe there is a lesson learning experience available to you. I do not know of any time or any place you can go in the Universe where learning is not available. This is true on the planet and outside the planet. It is also true in all the astral traveling that is done. Nothing is there just because it is there.

There is a lesson teaching function that becomes even more evident when you talk about earth or some of the other planets in this particular solar system. The whole purpose of being here is to provide a learning function to the inhabitants of the globe, and the only reason you come to this particular spot is to fulfill the necessary learning experience in this particular classroom. You have been to others. In fact, you have been around since infinity, and you will be around throughout infinity. You will go on to other 'classrooms' but you will undoubtedly be stuck here for quite a while. However, sooner or later there will be other places to go, other classrooms, and other conditions that have to be covered.

Often times you hear some thoughts about the end of the world coming and it is time to repent. The end of this world is not coming until the planet fulfills its requirement as a classroom. When there are no longer experience factors to be gained at this particular spot, earth is no longer needed. The planet will probably not even be inhabited at that particular time because, like a school, it would have graduated all of its students. There would no longer be any need for the planet, in which case it would go out of existence.

As long as the planet is here, it has to provide a definite classroom experience. This becomes the involved experience we know as life. What is most often missed is that earth is a very intricate classroom at this particular point. For a long time, I believed people when they would say that earth was the garbage can of the Universe. Then I went to Tibet and started to study. I found out things are not bad at all. This is not elementary work. There is a wide range of problems that are hard to encompass in our very involved postgraduate curriculum. We have come into a very difficult school. However, once we leave here and have the lesson experience learned, we are not going to have to worry about coming back to *this type* of intricate school. What makes it intricate? It has to work on three levels of awareness that are the spiritual, the mental, and the physical. These are levels that we face in our everyday life. We have a spiritual awareness, a psychological or mental awareness, and a physical awareness to live up to, and I am going to expand upon these.

One of the great problems in teaching (and in learning) in this area is that the minute you get a nucleus you have to go and expand and expand and expand upon it. One door just leads to another hallway with yet another door. There is never a point where you arrive with all the answers. You just keep going through more and more doors. It is true that by no means is it the end of learning about the subterranean society after my comments on the subject. If you want to take it further, we could go further and spend weeks, months, and years taking this subject, on and on and on.

What you *do* know about the levels of physical, mental, and spiritual is fine. Just know that I am going to expand and go on from there. The three levels of learning experiences exist more than to just exist on top of the surface of the earth as you know it. It is true that you are involved in these three levels in a small manner, but in the larger picture they fall into different categories. You actually have three levels of learning experience connected to this planet, with the first one being the spiritual level. The spiritual element does not actually exist on the planet itself. It exists as a learning experience in an etheric level *around* the planet. We know it in mysticism as the place you go when you die – the etheric world.

When you die, you don't take a trip off to Never-Never-Land. Your learning experience continues in the etheric world in this particular spiritual level of awareness. It is part and parcel of the trilogy of experience you have to have with Planet Earth. This is why the whole system of reincarnation is a fact and not a fallacy. Unless you have a learning reason to leave this area completely and take up residence at some other point within this galaxy, you can be assured your learning experience falls within this area. In other words, your etheric area is still allied to and attached to this planet when you die.

There is no way to fulfill the learning requirements of this planet until you fulfill these three areas <u>with the exception of the subterranean society.</u> It has basic requirements all its own, and there is no point in which we can say that the subterranean society is going to end. Not all of you touched into this subterranean society, nor do all of you need to touch into it on this planet. No matter where you go in the Universe, you only need to go through the subterranean level once. The first bodies on Planet Earth had a sense of form, which they manifested into a physical body. It is the etheric body that is the progression of a form experience which consciousness already had. This is not the same system that occurs for those needing the subterranean society orientation.

When you agreed to incarnate, it was your choice but your agreement is on a spiritual level. You agree on the basis of everything you know spiritually. In the final movement downward into the birth position, your spiritual awareness becomes less and less. You become more and more adapted to the physical awareness. Then when consciousness enters the body, it is not spiritually aware. It is physically aware. Its natural reaction is to try to get back out again, but it settles down and sticks it out. Again, this is not the same system that occurs for those needing the subterranean society orientation.

The Earth Plane

The so-called mental level actually exists on the earth plane itself. I don't think this is too difficult to understand. If you take an aware look at your life, your problems really don't seem to be spiritual or physical. They *do* appear to be mental: the worries, the ability to deal with people, the ability to cope with yourself. The list is a mile long. The mental frequency is the prime lesson on the crust of the earth. Of course there is an overlap into the spiritual, and you must include it. However, the prime level of activity is the mental level.

What you actually have is a system something like this: Draw a circle with the spiritual level surrounding the circle. Put the mental level in the middle with the physical level drawn as a circle inside the mental circle. The inside circle is the level we are going to explore in this lecture. What you are actually doing on the surface plane of the earth is to act as the middle point to hold the two elements, spiritual and physical, together. As I already indicated, there is an overlap. You are learning a great deal out of the spiritual and physical areas, but you are not learning <u>totality</u> out of either one because on the crust of the earth you cannot work <u>totally</u> in all three areas – only within the one mental area.

I know this is going to seem confusing to some who thought, up until now, that you could learn the spiritual, mental, and physical on the surface of the planet. More than anything else, you have to learn at the point of the mental area on the surface of the earth. This is what takes us from the etheric spiritual level to the mental earth level.

Then we move to the physical level. This is what we have in the subterranean society. That is where the physical elements are learned. There is no other place to learn them.

To begin with, there are only a certain number of planets at this point in the Universe that have physical manifestation. We happen to be one of them. There are a few others, but there are not a lot of them. There are planets that have only spiritual activity, and there are some that only have mental activity or a combination of the two. There are some that have only physical activity. The reason Planet Earth is intricately involved as a classroom is because it does encompass the three elements of the spiritual, mental, and physical levels within its requirement as a classroom.

The subterranean society is built on the physical plane learning experience <u>alone</u>. When I indicate physical, I am talking about the body as the lower element of the physical plane. For all the functioning you do on this plane inside the physical body, you are fairly well advanced – believe it or not! Regardless of your aches and pains, your headaches or being overweight, you are still fairly well advanced. I am not referring to you here and now. I am referring to certain types of consciousness who need to develop the ability to adjust to a purely physical environment. There is that necessity on Planet Earth.

Since the majority of planetary points in this part of the Universe (wherever this point might be) are not physical, most of the spiritual consciousness that we know as individuals who arrive on this planet have not had *any* physical experience. Consider what this would mean if I took you out of the Universe after fifty million years of experience. During those fifty million years, you had never had a physical form of any kind. You had never had a physical experience. Your experience has always been purely spiritual, purely mental, or a combination of those two – never physical. Then I shove you into the limitation of a physical body and I say, "Here. Have at it. You are now alive on Planet Earth. Go through your experiences." That is absolutely impossible. You couldn't do it. There is no way that consciousness could adjust. You wouldn't even know how to operate the body and, above all, you wouldn't know how to operate within the physical laws of the planet itself.

In a number of life readings that I do in my work, there are people who come into incarnations on this planet who have been away from the planet for a long time, but they have had physical experiences. They just may not have incarnated for three, four, or eight thousand years or maybe fifteen or twenty thousand years by man-made time. Then, they return as children in a physical body. They find it so miserably hard to adjust that, in many cases, they spend most of their life trying to get out of it. When it shows up in a life reading that the person has had that kind of experience, I can be sure ninety-nine times out of one hundred that the individual's birth was difficult. The spirit tried to get out at the last minute. Usually the birth was hard, the baby was ill and sometimes an incubator was necessary because of the resistance of the consciousness to be put into the limitations of a physical body.

Adjustment Period

The body is a great machine, but to an outsider operating with the freedom of movement that only consciousness can give you, it is like being put into a very unfavorable and difficult prison. Consider the individual who has not had any experience in a body. If you were to throw consciousness into a body, the body could not maintain it, nor could it function in the basic care of itself. With all of the background, power, and energy consciousness has had, it would not even consider staying inside the unit itself. It would do something in some way to get out of it and to rid itself of the body.

On this planet there must be a basic adjustment period in the physical area that takes place. That adjustment period cannot take place on the surface of the planet. It must take place in some area basically isolated from the spiritual and mental part of the classroom that we have here. That place is the subterranean region of the earth itself, which is located somewhere in the vicinity of thirty-five to fifty miles below the earth's crust, deep into the earth. There are some caves in and around the New Mexico area that have no bottom. There are also a few in Kentucky. These so-called caves are some of the inlets that would go down as far as the subterranean area, but there is no way of getting to that depth. The number of twists and turns at the different levels makes it impossible to reach. Nevertheless, some of the openings do lead, if you could follow them down, into that particular point. Some of these cave-type points are in Europe and some in northern Germany. There are a few areas in Spain and a number of them in the Himalayas where the caves actually have no end. You go into the caves and suddenly they drop down indefinitely.

What we are dealing with here is what we call a first touchdown of a spirit who must begin to orient to the planet in order to live here. In those situations, the first touchdown has to be made in the subterranean area. I must point out that this does not apply to all of you, and (in most cases) it doesn't apply to any of you. You have had basic physical experiences elsewhere before your arrival on this planet. Therefore, your arrival here was getting into a body through a very normal birth and functioning in that body. As a matter of fact, in all the decades of years I have done life readings, I have only found three individuals who have had experience in the subterranean society and are still here on the planet. It is not a common experience you will find at our particular level.

The touchdown into the subterranean society has only one basic need. That need is for the adjustment of consciousness into a physical body. If you have not gone through this necessary adjustment (or if you have not been aware of this up close as some of us have by certain experiences), it is very difficult for you to understand the tremendous problem it is to get the consciousness *to operate* the body. This is not just taking care to feed yourself. This pertains to operating something as basic as the movements of the body. In the body's main encasement, the main object of consciousness is to get out and not to stay in. Therefore, consciousness tries very hard to throw off the body instead of learning how it functions.

Remember, your body doesn't function out of the nervous system or out of the brain system by itself. It is animated by consciousness and energy *with* the function *through* the nervous system using the brain as a mechanical device. As many of you have already determined, you can project the consciousness out of the body, and the body will stay in some suspended function while you can go on and do other things in consciousness alone. What is needed here in the adjustment period is this so-called *lock-in* as a means to make it work. This leads us to the kind of physical body that has to be used to allow for this. In other words, what do we have here in the subterranean society?

Single Functioning Unit

First, there is no male or female gender. There is just one single functioning unit that has no reproductive capability. The reason for this is that its functioning is not on a mental or spiritual level. In order to give it any reproductive capability, it is going to have to have emotion. It doesn't have emotion. The minute you give it emotion, you have immediately elevated it from the physical level into the mental or psychological area. That would make the functioning at the subterranean level no longer valid, so this is denied the consciousness in order to get it enclosed in the encasement of the body.

Since the body does not have reproductive functions, the next obvious question arises about how the bodies got there and what happened. The so-called life span in the subterranean society runs somewhere between ten and twenty-five years. With very few exceptions, it is hardly longer. The arrival at this particular point is done on what we call astral incubation. That is about the only name I can give it. Let's assume we have a subterranean body working already. When the consciousness has oriented itself enough to function *with* the physical encasement in a proper way – that is through a normal system of nerves – it has completed its first basic lesson experience on the planet. At this point, the individual is no longer required to remain at the subterranean society level. It departs.

The individual goes into a cave-like area and lies down. The system goes through something we would assume as a death. Consciousness is withdrawn from the subterranean body, and the physical function stops. Consciousness returns to the spiritual etheric area and is now ready at some future time to make its first incarnation on the planet's surface. It will receive its first orientation on the surface in the emotional and mental areas. It does not ever return to the subterranean level. All it needed was to go through that level once. It received all it needed from that level because it would not leave the subterranean level until it learned how to function in the physical body.

When consciousness is withdrawn at the point of death, there is no deterioration of the body in the subterranean society. It is immediately inhabited by another consciousness that takes over for a short incubation period. The body doesn't get up and say, "Okay, here I am. Let's go." Consciousness is held in something of a suspended animation for a short period of time. This short period of time can run from two to three months or maybe as long as eight months. There is a *lock-in* here, and consciousness is fighting the body all of this time. When consciousness begins to become aware that it is in a physical vehicle, it becomes aware of the necessity to move it. Very slowly and very clumsily the body gets up, leaves the area of incubation, and begins its first operation in the subterranean society. In this change over, there isn't any need for the normal perpetuation of reproduction that we have because reproduction doesn't operate on that particular basis. Therefore, the population in the subterranean society is constant without ever increasing or decreasing.

Population

When Planet Earth took its place in space, a complete blueprint of its whole operation came along with it. In the original blueprint, there was a determination as to what the population of the subterranean society should be. The size of the planet sets that determined size. Obviously, you are not going to have a subterranean society of seventy-two billion people on a planet this size. The planet's blueprint includes all three areas made up of the subterranean area, the mental surface area, and the so-called spiritual or etheric area.

We continue to fulfill that blueprint. That is all we are doing. Of course in so doing, we are fulfilling ourselves. You might say that this is destiny and we cannot get out of it. No, that is not true. You make your own destiny. The modifications are made in your own life. However, the planet itself has a blueprint, and the blueprint is set for the well being of the planet. The planet's blueprint is perfect, as is everything in the Universe. The determination from its very beginning is to its ultimate, whatever that may be. Then it is no longer needed as a classroom.

There are only certain levels and certain spots within the interior of the planet that can sustain the subterranean society. That determination is made according to the size of the planet that is set by the diameter of the globe, more than anything else. The limitations are set right there. The population set for the subterranean society runs to about one and three-quarter million. That is about the best figure I have ever been able to pick up on it, and it is considered a relatively low factor in the whole scheme of things. You can see that the amount of in-coming consciousness that need to readjust in the subterranean society is not very many by comparison to the number of people who are born on the planet under normal conditions.

There is obviously no childhood because of the astral incubation. The population is constant. You must remember that there is no emotional upset at this level, at all. There is no pain, no fear, no crying, and no being happy; none of the emotions we feel exist at this particular level. That is not the function of the subterranean level.

Physical Features

The physical features of the subterranean people have some very definitive differences from ours. The features are so gross that you can hardly define them. They could not be considered very pretty by our standards. In many respects, they are not ugly either. In describing their physical features, I need to emphasize that these are not ape-like people. Their bodies are marked by a lack of hair because there is no need for the warmth hair provides. The average size of the person is between five feet six inches and five feet ten inches. Their heads are extremely large in size. This is necessary in order for the consciousness to learn how to function in the mechanical device called the brain. You can say, if it has a brain it has a nervous system, and if it has a nervous system it has got to have emotional feelings. It does have functioning, but it doesn't have feelings in that sense.

There is very little need for eyes. What we know as eyes are very, very small, but there is a great need for air so the nostrils of the nose are very large for the intake of air. This is in order for consciousness to learn how to function by breathing. Remember, consciousness has had no experience functioning in a physical body. The mouth area is very small because the whole digestive process is not a necessity. Hunger is an emotion. The so-called body of the subterranean person does not get hungry with hunger pangs because the body is nourished under normal conditions, without the necessity of having the feeling of hunger.

The ears are relatively large because there must be a sensation of awareness into the brain function. The neck is large enough to support the extremely large head, but where the body really differs is in the upper torso. It has an enormously wide back, as if you are looking at a block of granite. The chest is wide and very deep to allow for the function of breathing in air. They live primarily on what we would call manna. They live out of the air for their food. I am going to go off on a tangent for a moment. The individuals who return to the earth without much physical experience are the worst eaters in the world. They have very odd eating habits because they are not use to eating, nor do they want to eat. Picky. Picky. Picky. You cannot please these people with food.

The lower part of the torso is narrow. Since there is a very limited function of excretion and no sexual function, it isn't necessary to have a large interior area. It narrows down in that region and, oddly enough, goes into very large thick legs. The size of the large calf is equal to the size of the thigh with a very, very thick ankle. The joints in the ankle are also very large. One of the problems in consciousness taking over this unit is the instability. This is compensated for by the use of these heavy legs and very wide feet in order to give stability. The feet are about two-and-half times the width of our feet but about the same length. The arms are shapeless but not large, and the hands and fingers are half again as large as ours. Manipulation of all the joints is very clumsy.

Aging Indicators

We have balance and we have dexterity. We know how to keep ourselves balanced. At this particular level, they don't. As it gets nearer to their time to leave the society (whenever that happens to be) the dexterity increases. However, the body does not change, and there is no refinement in the body. It is just that the ability to operate it becomes better. You see some of these individuals moving around at a very rapid rate by comparison, and you will see some literally waddling. That is how you can tell age. The slower ones have not been there long, and the faster ones have been there a longer period of time. When you see a pretty fast movement in comparison to others, you know they are about ready to leave. When we are going to die, we slow down. When they are going to die, they speed up. This is pretty good juxtaposition.

Atmosphere

The areas they inhabit are very warm because of being fifty some miles into the depth of the earth. They are actually heated as a result of certain mineral compounds that we have not discovered. The minerals are not close enough to the surface of the earth for us to unearth, but they are something like uranium. Obviously, this is not uranium, but the minerals do throw off a radioactive substance, which does perform the function of heat. The area is very, very warm and the atmosphere remains constant. There is no clothing because there isn't a need for clothing.

There is water. There are water deposits at these deep levels, and they are used by the functions of the bodies. I think in years to come, science is going to discover a great deal of water under earth's crust. There is vegetation somewhat like ours. The selection is limited because it is not needed. The air is heavy like it is in the Midwest after a thunderstorm. You can smell the ozone like you can after lightening hits. In the subterranean levels you can smell the ozone. It is the ozone levels that keep the bodies from deteriorating and aging. In fact, connected with the ozone are the DNA and RNA factors that provide the life giving force. I don't know what to call it besides air - maybe atmosphere. Their lighting is an auric-type phosphorescence. However, lighting is not a necessity; that is why the eyes are small in the whole function of the system. The individuals don't have any great use for eyes. They don't read and there isn't any television!

Socialization

As much as it may be distasteful to you, there is no social functioning at all. They are not led, and they are not organized. If anything, they form together as groups or units for no reason at all. There is no mental function at this particular level so there is no need for socializing. <u>Remember:</u> Their whole period is just to learn how to orient to the body and use it. That is a big job. That is all they do all day long. All that is being done during the whole period is learning how to motivate the body, how to move, how to sit, how to kneel, how to squat, how to bend over, how to walk properly, how to move the arms, how to get dexterity out of the fingers, and how to get mobility into the wrists. They do a great deal of walking and moving about. There are sleep periods. There is no mental stimulation because there is no need for communication. They have no emotional impact on one another, one way or another. All knowledge is physical knowledge in which the consciousness is learning about itself.

Astral Visits

I took a journey into this area on an astral basis. Astral projection is based upon your knowledge, your experience, and your association with your astral associates. No one will tell you where you can and cannot go. It was suggested that I not take the first trip alone. This astral trip was going down, not up and away. There is quite an adjustment of energy that is necessary to move through a solid mass of material. In my particular situation, I had to have an associate from the astral area who had made the trip and who knew how to adjust the vibratory level in consciousness that is woven through to the fifty mile limit. I did not know how to readjust to that level. When you go out into the Universe, you ramp up in your frequency, but going down into these areas you tune down. It is harder to tune down your frequency and keep it under control than it is to crank it up.

The first group I came upon was rather comical. They were sitting in an oblong circle, but they all had their back to the center of the circle looking outward. The only thing I could figure out that had taken place was that one individual sat down and another one came along and saw this position. Maybe the person had never tried it. By a certain amount of visual imitation, the person imitated and began learning how to physically function in that way. The next individual came along, saw that position, and sat down facing outward also. Eventually, there was a whole group of them all facing outward and not communicating. Some sitting there may have been there five years and others who came along maybe two or three years. The ones sitting down showed the others a new thing to do, but not in the sense of leadership. As they become effective in running the body, they set an example to others by seeing what another does. They don't lead anyone. There is no emotional play that is involved. I see you and by natural instinct I walk toward you.

They do have an auric energy. I don't want to say it is pathetic, but it is very upsetting because these individuals are each a fantastic consciousness that has been locked into this system in order to train them. Reading the auric energy, you get extremely brilliant individuals who have spent millions (possibly billions) of centuries completely free of physical resistance. Looking into it, you have something really beautiful but, in another way, sad because the consciousness is locked into the body as a training process. They come in from experiences in which they had no bodies at all. They come in as consciousness, as formless energy, without any shape. They didn't have any need for form. When they have met their learning requirement and leave the subterranean society, they go into the spiritual area in what we can call *an observation of the crust purpose.* This experience aligns their basic learning function in the gross body to the more advanced function necessary to incarnate on the earth's surface. Their discarnate experience is generally under seventy-five years.

One Step Up

You need to understand that this is the only reasonable process to train the consciousness. You cannot be trained in anything in the Universe without experience. I can tell you everything I know and it is nice knowledge. However, when you take one step of experience, it will mean much more. You have had an experience. You are involved.

Part II
Alien Territory

> *The planet is not a natural home for consciousness.*
> *--GT*

Let's see if we can put ourselves on a like-thought pattern by looking at how it is consciousness maintains a continuity of life force as an element that comes out of the Universe and belongs to the Universe. Then let's bring this down to earth by considering the whys, the hows, and the wherefores of the physical body that is run under the nature kingdom and is representative *from* the planet. We are going to begin by considering the roles of consciousness. Characteristically, consciousness is the same as the expression of Universal intelligence at Its smallest point. It has no form, but it does have some very definite characteristics.

Life Force

1. <u>Consciousness has continuity</u>. The problem with the Universe is Its enormity and Its infinity. Anything that is infinite can never know itself because it is forever infinitely aware of an infinite amount that never stops. Therefore, the way the Universe finds its elements is by giving the same quality of awareness to its parts. The parts in the Universe are called consciousness. How many are there? An infinite number. Do they come into being and go out of being? No. Like the Universe, they have always been. There has always been the Universe, and there has always been consciousness. If we were to isolate you as one of these units in consciousness (and we can), you have always been. Your

infinity maintains the continuity of life force in the Universe by virtue of a continuity of experience.

The Universe knows Itself by the fact that the parts go through experiences. For instance, you can tell a lot about a car if you take the engine apart and look at the parts of the engine. You can tell just how efficient the engine is and how hard that engine was run by the parts that are worn. In a more refined sense, the Universe can tell about Its history by the fact that consciousness carries the experience and the continuity. The first act of consciousness is to maintain this sense of life continuity, experience after experience, wisdom after wisdom, and intelligence after intelligence, ad infinitum.

The big cry metaphysically has always been, "If I am this in consciousness, how come I am not terribly bright and able to do all of this?" You are. You just don't know how to get to it. In some cases, in getting to it you can't stand the power involved. Nothing has ever been denied to you. It is just that you continue to run back to what you consider some safe, familiar place. What you need to remember is that we are talking about wisdom. We are not talking about intelligence in terms of learning details, but wisdom is very hard for me to put my finger on because it is essence. It is not tangible. It is knowing without knowing how you know. How do you know how you know? You don't know how you know. You just know. That is essence. In many cases you find that too intangible.

If I pose a problem to you, you would immediately start to solve it. If you were in touch with consciousness, you wouldn't start to solve it because you know it is already solved. The answer, if there is an answer at all, is already there. The only thing you have to do is to say, "It is there." You don't do that, and there are reasons you don't do that.

2. <u>Consciousness stores wisdom</u>. It acts as a very valuable, important, and efficient storage unit. The Universe doesn't store knowledge. Consciousness stores knowledge of the Universe. In other words, the parts store the knowledge. Go back to breaking down the engine of the car. It's the parts that tell you whatever transpired in that engine. The same thing applies to the Universe. Consciousness becomes the recorder for the Universe by storing the material. How does the Universe know Itself? It knows Itself because Its parts store all this information. Since the Universe is a totality, It simply *feels* Its parts. You know when you are feeling well because all the cells in your body feel well. Your cells give you a message that you don't pay any attention to, but you feel good. You feel ill by your cells giving you the opposite message. It's your individual cells that tell you that you don't feel well, or that you are under stress, or that you feel great. The way you know how you feel is by putting all those messages together.

Consciousness stores all this material and It does not have a problem with volume. It can store infinitely. You ask, "If my consciousness stores infinitely, why can't I go back to billions and billions of experiences ago and pull those out?" It isn't that you can't. What value is doing that to you on this planet at this moment? There just isn't any value and application to do that here and now. By virtue of where you are, you are somewhat blocked from doing that type of thing. This is a self-inflicting safety valve on the part of consciousness. Since the Universe does not waste Its knowledge, why give knowledge where it can't be used?

3. <u>Consciousness is also the keeper of the will</u>. Will is a characteristic of the Universe that produces action and motion, and you cannot have action without will presaging the action. What is will? Will is an indefinable universal energy that has infinite manifestations. We know that will

must exist in order to produce some action, but we cannot say that will is tantamount to desire. Desire is there because of want, but in the Universe there is no want so will stands on its own. It is not produced by desire. It is consciousness that is the keeper of the will by holding on to the ability to initiate that will into action and that action is not predicated upon any lack. It is predicated upon what consciousness wants to express.

4. <u>Consciousness sustains Universal Law.</u> It supports the whole by supporting Universal Law in all of its out workings.

Look at all these unique things that we really are in consciousness. We are everything the Universe is, could be, or would ever want to be. Even before I start talking about consciousness as an alien element living inside the body on this planet, you have to realize we are in a lot of trouble. What we have is this little encapsulation of the Universe (consciousness) living in only a small infinitesimal corner of the room. How can consciousness maintain a continuity of life force, store wisdom, be the keeper of the will, and sustain the Universal Law in all of its out workings? The very first thing you should see is that the characteristics of consciousness are so great that how could we even presume to let it encapsulate in a little body compared to all it is! It's like entrapping a beautiful stallion into the space one-half the size of a horse. Therein lays an enormous problem.

Of course consciousness belongs here as part of its experience. It is here willingly by virtue of its own will, and it carries with it all the stored wisdom that it has. What it doesn't have is the arena in which it can use and put out all of this energy and this knowledge. It just has a different methodology by which it has to exist.

Earth Body

Now we have to turn to the body. From this point on, I want your concept of the physical body to be the nature of the planet (Mother Nature, if you like). I want those two words to be interchangeable - nature and the body. They are to be understood as one and the same thing.

1. <u>The root characteristic of this particular planet is that it is female</u>. Every celestial body has definite root characteristics. It is a receptive womb, and it produces a mothering, nurturing base. This is why everything on the planet is in family units. There is the family of trees, the family of animals, and the family of humans. Everything comes out of a creative mode and disappears to create in another mode as a creative-oriented experience. Nothing here is lost. We burn a log and it becomes ashes. The ashes turn into something else. Everything on the planet is created new, just as everyday a certain number of cells in your body die. They disappear externally and internally, but they don't die off and disappear into nothingness. They are immediately replaced into the creative cycle, just as the phoenix bird rises out of the fire in its own ashes.

We live on one of the most abundant physical planets that you are ever likely to see. Wherever you go there is something that nurtures and manifests into something real and tangible. I find that people have the hardest time to grasp the idea that the planet is manifesting. Consequently, their life means nothing unless they are manifesting. The greatest idea in the world is worthless until the idea becomes tangible because this planet will never allow anything to exist for an indefinite period of time without it coming into manifestation. If you are an angry, hateful person, that anger and hate will manifest whether you try to hide it or not. In the same respect, if you are warm, loving person that will manifest even if you do nothing to point out that is what you are. It will still manifest. You can't keep things on this planet from happening, and that is what you don't like. You ask why so many things happen that appear to be very difficult and negative. Metaphysically, we say they happen because you brought them into being. There is no way you could hold back the manifestation. One of the keys in learning how to get along here, unusually well, is to remember that, whether you like it or not, it is going to manifest. Since you can't stop it, you might as well set it up in a very positive sense so it starts manifesting all the positive things.

2. <u>The planet is also a change-maker.</u> Nothing on this planet will remain stable. It must change, and we are not talking about a change next year or in the next decade. This planet is in change every micro-millisecond of time. This causes one of the greatest problems because, by their very nature, people generally do not want to change. They find themselves threatened by change and incapable of dealing with it. It's almost as if they are trying to get the planet to stop, but it won't stop and it can't stop.

Your body is in constant change moment-to-moment. It is getting older. There is deterioration, a settling, and a wearing taking place. You know as many people as I do who design their lives to try to prevent the change, but you are never going to get younger. You will always get older. Nevertheless, that does not mean older and incapacitated. It means change, and you can change into a whole new thing. It happens in nature all the time in very visual and obvious ways with the animals getting rid of their fur, the snakes shedding their skins, the trees losing their leaves, and the butterflies emerging out of their cocoons. The cycles change but we generally tend to ignore these changes.

Interior Alien

Let's bring this down to a point of what we have here in consciousness whose elements are continuity, wisdom, will, and Law. Those are the words that I use. Do you see anything very tangible in those elements? You have consciousness in a vehicle on a planet that is mothering, creative, nurturing, manifesting, and changing. You have two different elements involved here. Continuity can be part of the experience, but part of what experience? Wisdom can be part of the experience but what experience? In other words, you really can't match up continuity, wisdom, will, and Law to the basic characteristic elements of the planet.

You are an alien in an alien place. You are sitting there with an interior alien inside of you but not alien in the sense that consciousness immediately wants to withdraw. Consciousness must adapt to wherever it finds itself. Even though consciousness recognizes this is an alien atmosphere, it cannot interfere with the physical laws of nature. A great deal of metaphysical activity and work has been focused on the fact that if you get a hold of consciousness you can change everything in your life. No, you can't! You *can* work with what you have got here and make the most out of it, but you cannot usurp natural law or change it on this planet. The planet was out of universal design and creativity, and the Universe cannot turn one element of Itself against another element of Itself. That is inconsistent. The Universe will never send anything It creates to overcome Itself. The planet was created with a natural law. There is no way that consciousness, in any form on this planet, can come and change and capture that natural law.

It is terribly important that you come to the realization that this is not a very comfortable place for you. It never will be in the sense that it is not a natural home for the consciousness.

Consciousness is uncomfortable here and it does feel out of place. It does not look upon the planet as a warm, comfortable, secure little niche that it can enjoy for seventy, eighty, or one-half million years. It looks at it as being a very alien and hostile environment. However, it is not trying to usurp, change, or conquer the body or natural laws of the planet.

It is your body that belongs to the planet. It finds the environment perfectly okay because every element in your body belongs to nature. It came from the planet, and it is going to return to the elements of the planet. Everything in your body can be found in the animal, vegetable, and minerals of the planet. Everything in the planet can be found in your body. Your body works according to the laws of nature, responds to the laws of nature, functions to the laws of nature, and develops to the laws of nature. I need to emphasize that the master of the body is the planet; the body does not respond at all to consciousness.

For years, decades, and maybe centuries, metaphysicians have come along and tried to sell the other theme in which consciousness controls the body. Experience will tell you that never works. There is no such thing as mind over matter. There is matter over matter. Consciousness isn't the least bit interested in being in control or changing anything here. If we were to isolate consciousness and ask it how it would like to change this life, it would answer, "What life?" We would say, "Well, you know, the one you are in." The response from consciousness would be, "I am not in any life. What I am doing is registering an experience. I don't know what you are talking about." It refuses and refutes the body. It will not take any responsibility for it. Therefore, consciousness is not in a position to critique the body and it doesn't. It *is* in a position to support Universal Law and to store wisdom.

Now we turn to another point. We <u>know</u> we have consciousness because that is who we are. That is our continuity into infinity. We <u>know</u> that consciousness finds itself in a vehicle that belongs to this planet. Therefore, we know that consciousness is in an alien space. What we should realize, whether we like it or not, is that we truly are individualized units operating in one point of mass. That is consciousness does exist, the body does exist, they both belong to us, and we have to operate two units as one unit.

Good news – bad news. The good news is that we can address ourselves to a broad range of categories. One category is in consciousness and one category is physical. However, to get those two units to work together is a *real* hassle. They do not fight each other because consciousness is not in control of the body and the body is not in support of consciousness. So how are you going to get them in a position where they can understand each other and cooperate? We are asking for the most unusual of conditions to take place without having either the knowledge or the wisdom to know what to do. This is why the world is in such turmoil most of the time.

Let's go back to some basics. Consciousness doesn't give a nitpicker's damn in hell what you do with this life or any other life you are going to have here. It does not care what you do in life because it does not design the life. Life, as we know it, belongs to the planet, which is the element in manifestation. But consciousness is an observer (a registrar, if you like). It is a historian. It is your conscience as the voice on your shoulder reminding you that the Universe still exists. For example, consciousness says, "Let's go to that school (meaning earth) because I want to learn relationships." Now, how many ways are there of learning relationships? I don't know. Consciousness doesn't really care *how* it is going to learn relationships as long as it learns <u>in relationship to what it wants to store as wisdom</u>.

It knows what its needs are because it is always aware of itself. *I have gone through all my records of all my books and what I need here is some experience about relationships. There's a good school. We'll go to that one.*

In terms of working out the experience at that particular point, consciousness has no idea what is going to happen. That is why we have the Reincarnation Board. That is why we have other individuals mapping out what apparently are physical plans and blueprints because consciousness doesn't want to do it. If we didn't have a physical blueprint, consciousness would just sit there observing and the body would revert back to the planet. That would be very animalistic and very basic. We are pretty basic anyhow. We have to eat. We tend to fight for our life as a matter of survival. We eliminate. We propagate. We change, we grow, and we die. This is just as basic as any animal group in the jungle.

However, the difference is that inside the human body is an individualized consciousness. That is what makes the body unique, but the consciousness is not doing anything to overcome, to change, or to direct that life. All it does is carry the record. If you want to attach a word to it so you feel comfortable, let's say it is your 'conscience'. It is that angel on your shoulder that reminds you that you are, in truth, universal and part of the Universe. Therefore, all the Laws of the Universe apply, but consciousness does not make those Laws apply here.

In the same category, the body ignores the consciousness. The body sees consciousness as an alien. Its attitude is, "I don't know what you are doing here, but I am not going to listen to you. You don't belong here. You don't belong as part of my family. I don't see any of my characteristics in you." Your body is *always* looking at the planet and never beyond the planet. If you talked about meditation as a <u>meta</u>physical action, none of your body is involved. Your body does not look at 'meta-action' anything. It only looks at physical action. Without that you would have people seeing one another on non-physical levels and there isn't any attraction force on non-physical levels. Consciousness does not attract other consciousness in that way. Otherwise, you would have consciousness 'bodies' banging into each other and exploding.

Physical bodies are attracted within the same laws that apply to animals in their season. As interested developers and metaphysicians, it behooves you to start learning that you have to live with this somewhat competitive situation. Stop believing that consciousness is going to change the physical law of nature or that nature is going to change consciousness. <u>That is simply not true.</u> You are a split personality. You must devote a certain amount of time to your consciousness and a certain amount of time to your body.

However, the ratio is not equal. By and large, hardly anyone devotes any time to consciousness. Therefore, the Universe (knowing this and knowing this is an alien space) set in a safety valve. The safety valve is that every night, *every night,* consciousness withdraws from the body. This can be anywhere from a micro-millisecond to a few minutes, and it is usually during your sleep-state. However, you don't have to be asleep for consciousness to refurbish itself at the universal fountain and come back in again. You can be driving your car and you will be completely withdrawn for a fraction of the time when the consciousness goes out to refurbish. This happens to every living human being regardless of race, creed, color, and location. This happens every single period of twenty-four hours.

You can see that if you don't want to pay much attention to consciousness, it will take care of itself anyway. Obviously ninety-nine percent of the load here is the physical load. It is the body responding to nature and still carrying on with its experience. You can turn around and say, "Well, is a life learning lesson a lesson for the body or for consciousness?" It is a lesson for the body, but it is historical for consciousness. See the difference?

Consciousness doesn't have to go through the experience. It has to record it. It has to have the knowledge as an experience, but it is not involved in the experience. Your cells have the experience. Consciousness has the wisdom without knowing of the experience. If I took your consciousness out of you and I asked it to tell me about your past life and background experience, your consciousness would say, "Huh? What? I didn't have any life."

Consciousness knows about the wisdom it has, but it cannot identify experience since it doesn't have experience, just as the Universe has wisdom and cannot identify experience. It *is* experience. You are kidding yourself as you go through your physical opportunities here and say, "Well, I must be consciously aware and my consciousness is learning this and my consciousness is learning that." That is not what is happening at all.

Your body and the tens of billions of cells in your body are going through an experience. You have to pay attention to the action, the pain, the joy – whatever – and that is usually the exact area you want to ignore. Somewhere along the line, you have developed the sensation that being physical is too mundane. You are all aware of consciousness, and you know that there is a higher element. Nevertheless, you come up with all these excuses of why you don't want to participate. "Look at these unhappy people.

Look at their world that is in such a mess. Look at what nature does." It is always in a negative form rather than realizing it is all very positive. Nature does not pollute itself. We pollute nature. Nature is a non-polluter. Does consciousness bring destruction? No. We bring destruction.

You must understand that here you are in your duality with an alien inside of you that really doesn't give you any particular support. Experience is a body element. This is one reason I stress taking care of the body. You must coordinate with nature because consciousness isn't going to keep you alive. Consciousness *is* alive. It doesn't know death. If you said to consciousness, "I am dying. You have to keep me alive." Consciousness would answer, "I don't know what you are talking about. I am not dying."

The Will to Survive

If you have the will to live, it is the physical will to live. It is not a will of consciousness. Once you stop misaligning and misdirecting what you think you've got for support, you will find that living here is a lot more fun because you are responding to the planet and to nature as you should. You live with the war, the greed, the cruelty because you understand what the experience means. The experience is there as a present experience and does something for you to increase your awareness at a certain point, for a certain reason, and at a certain time. What counts is your experience even if you consider it minor (and there are a lot of minor ones) or major. They are all there for your physical experience at the moment.

The alien within, consciousness, is just observing the show. Consciousness is saying, "Gee, that's interesting. I'll mark that down." It is not helping you, changing you, nor is it supporting you. It is *already* in its perfection. It refurbishes you at the fountain of the Universe every single night. It does not care if you are going through any pain. This is why people who think there is some magic in metaphysics that can pay their rent, bring lovers, and change their lives are crazy! They are the ones who think, "The Universe will do this." It will not because the Universe (and consciousness as part of the Universe) doesn't even know what is going on in that sense. It is not there for that.

The will of survival is only in the body and consciousness thinks nothing of survival. That is why people who are very elderly and have lived a good life can sit back and not be upset about dying. They are now living more in the awareness of consciousness where there is no ending to this thing at all. You are mistaken if you set yourself up to tell yourself that you are communicating and transmitting between body and consciousness and also getting sustenance from consciousness. Such an attitude will work against you every time because you cannot get support on this planet except from nature. What is one of the qualities of nature? It is nourishing. Have you seen anyone on this planet existing without food for more than thirty-eight or thirty-nine days running? The body must take from the planet to sustain itself.

Conformity

Let's say you are facing a problem, a challenge, or an opportunity as an experience. Metaphysically (and unfortunately) your first inclination is to attack the situation through consciousness. Right there you are in trouble. This is why many times your initial output to an action falls flat on its face. To you, doing it spiritually means doing it by consciousness. Doing it spiritually to your body means doing it according to nature's law. That is spiritual – the spirit of nature. The spirits of nature are the wind, the sun, the trees, and the air. When you pray, you pray to the planet. Don't pray to the Universe except if you are going to move out of your body and work with your consciousness. In that case, the consciousness won't pray at all. It has nothing to pray for because it is already aware. It *is* awareness.

> The spiritual man* conforms to nature's law.
> The mental man conforms to nature's action.
> The physical man conforms to nature's need.

When you are conforming to your physical level, it is all needs and wants. It is sex, food, elimination, and health. When you are conforming to your mental level, it is the creative action on the part of nature. When you are conforming to your spiritual level, you are aware of and <u>using</u> (because this is all manifested) nature's law. You produce a manifestation. It all works out. You are not walking along as spiritual man....la, la, la. *I am up here and my feet are not on the ground.* That is not true at all. You are very much in touch with nature. You are applying its law.

How do you approach life and its experiences under these circumstances? In no way have I intended to communicate that you are meant to ignore the role of consciousness. After all, that is your connector and sustenance to the Universe. If you can allow and willingly spend time with consciousness (which is not meditation), you are in a state that is nothingness. It is everything. It is true that it is transcendental of nature, but I can't tell you what it is because it doesn't have any definition. It is knowing that I am without knowing that I am. The knowing is consciousness being back in touch with the Universe. It has no axe to grind. It has nothing to ask for.

---

* 'Man' is used generically to indicate all people.

It doesn't have anything to give. If you want to involve yourself with that, it is perfectly okay. There is nothing wrong with that, but if you don't want to spend your time that way, consciousness will refuel itself sometime within a twenty-four hour period anyway.

Nature's Law

What are you going to do with the other you that *must* produce the experience for consciousness to record and store the wisdom from the experience? Let's start with nature and the law – the spiritual man. The laws of nature include the law of gravity, the law of electricity, and all the physical laws that have been discovered, as well as, those that have yet to be discovered. What you need to be aware of is how you get along with nature and how you live according to nature's law, not about how to get along with partners and mates.

How do you live according to nature's law? The first, the foremost, and the easiest way is to pay attention to your body. Your body doesn't belong to you. The body belongs to the planet. It is *always* in touch with the planet. It senses every motion, every vortex, and every energy change. Your body picks up every condition of the planet. In order to feel this connection, you must be receptive and stop dictating and transmitting messages to your body. Remember that nature is a nurturing receptive element. Your state of mind (and mind has nothing to do with your consciousness) must be receptive. It is not giving out any messages at all. It just receives. It is not looking for anything or asking for anything.

Don't look heavenward for reception because nothing physical comes from heaven. If you try to transmit your need for two thousand dollars to heaven, you are in a lot of trouble! I've done as much traveling as I think anyone has in the heavenly realms, and I haven't seen a buck or anything that even comes close to it. Money is made here by people. It is material and physical. It can't come from heaven. Heaven can't even put money into motion. The response from consciousness would be, "Let's go where? And, what is two thousand dollars?" The reaction is only from the body. Your cells know because, in this case, it sees money as a form of sustenance and your body completely understands its needs for sustenance.

Let me illustrate this: It is a cold, freezing winter night. You are lost and have been traipsing through the snow when you come upon this cabin. You go inside knowing if you don't get out of the elements you are going to freeze to death. There is a magical genie inside the cabin who says to you, "Before you do anything, you have to make a choice. In this pile is one million dollars in paper money and in this other pile is firewood. You must choose one." Which one are you going to choose? You are freezing. You can burn a million dollars in paper money in no time at all. Isn't it obvious that it isn't the money you want? It is the warmth you want. A million dollars isn't going to keep you alive. That firewood will keep you alive. The point is that when you are harmonizing with nature and nature's laws you must know what it is that you want for survival. Meanwhile, consciousness is observing saying, "That is really interesting. Okay, I am going to write that down" distilling it all into wisdom but not remembering it, at all, as experience.

There is continuity by consciousness matching this up to other wisdom. Nature, by law, does not repeat itself. Repetition is a human element. The leaves on the tree are not the same leaves that were on the tree last year. They are *new* leaves. Any form of repetition in nature is a conclusion, ergo death. When we talk about the very elderly part of life, we revert back to being a child. The cycle is complete, and at that point you are talking death because the cycle will not allow itself to go into an exact repetition.

The requirement as a spiritual person is to align yourself to nature's law. You don't know nature's law other than the fact as it pertains to your body's transmission of nature's laws to you. That means you must be receptive. Receptivity means quieting yourself enough that you can hear what your body is telling you. Become aware enough so that you pay attention to what your body is telling you all of the time. That is your body's attunement to nature.

Nature's Action

The requirement as a mental, intellectual person is to align yourself to nature in terms of action. Once you align yourself to nature's law, you have to formulate a plan, a creative blueprint that moves you to the basic human elements of producing something. It is true that everything you give to the planet, the planet gives back to you. *Whatever you put into life you are going to get back.* You give the planet anger and you get anger back. You give it love and understanding and nature gives you love and understanding back.

This brings us to a very important point. Consciousness is not fighting you as an alien. It is simply willing to accept the experience and mark it down. It is *your* unwillingness to respond as a natural element to the planet that causes the disruption that you blame on consciousness. You can be put in the most ungodly of atmospheres in the worst human condition possible, and your consciousness will come through it without a mark on it because it doesn't pay any attention other than jotting the experience down as distilled wisdom. However, your body reacts totally.

The people who are not affected by human conditions are not using mind over matter. What they are doing is reverting to consciousness in which they are not (*they are not*) recording any experience. The body is having the experience, but consciousness is not recording the experience because the people have withdrawn to consciousness and they have no body awareness. All the body elements are shut down and none of the experience is being recorded. The experience is there, but it is a dead area as far as consciousness recording the experience for wisdom.

Here is how matter over matter works. You are meant to tell your body what it wants to do, rather than your body telling you. Your cells respond to an order. They cannot reject one. That is a control command and a control position. However, people who go through a great deal of psychological pain often revert to consciousness. In fact, we have so many of them that we build institutions for them and lock them up. They are in mental institutions largely because they are living in consciousness and are not recording any experience. One of the disasters about these institutions is that there are all these people who have a series of things wrong with them on every physical level, but they live on and on. Any one of us could die with even one of their conditions, but they go on and on and on because consciousness isn't recording the incident. The bodies are just existing in a natural reflective state of nature. They should have been dead years ago (considering their physical state) because they are not paying any attention to their planetary experience.

There is a method whereby you can decide not to endure any further pain. What you do is cut off all your life experience and draw back to consciousness. However, consciousness cannot kill the body because consciousness did not *make* the body. Therefore, it cannot kill your body. It has to wait for the body to go off on its own accord. The best way to control an obstreperous condition is to establish some base of fear. The obstreperous condition responds based on fear, and the way to produce fear on this planet is to produce a law that is higher than nature. That is what produced the concept of heaven and hell. Treated as a law, heaven and hell is above nature. That sets in the fear that if you don't do what 'they' say, you are going to have to answer to that higher law. The fact of the matter is that all of that is a lot of bunk. There is only one law on this planet. It is the law of nature.

The Law of Cause and Effect

You can't answer to a higher law because consciousness is the higher law. It answers to itself and always has answered to itself as a part of the Universe. Of course you have to pay for being negative and cruel, but you pay for it physically. You will come back and pay for it, and it will be physical. You are not going to pay for it in heaven or hell. Consciousness doesn't have to pay for it because it didn't <u>do</u> anything. **Karma has nothing to do with consciousness.** Karma is the law of cause and effect, and cause and effect is one of nature's laws. Every cause produces an effect, and every effect produces another cause.

In response to nature's law, we must manifest energy in order for it to become tangible and produce something in our physical lives. That is how we live and that is why we do not call upon this alien within for the so-called sustenance, which is often asked to run this life. It cannot and will not run this life for us.

Nature's Needs

Let's consider a few basics. It is essential for you to understand that this whole thing is run under the natural kingdom of the planet, and that the body is representative *from* the planet. Your body comes from the planet and belongs to it, and your consciousness sits within as an alien observing and recording. Your first requirement is to your body and to the health of your body. This does not mean just the way it looks. This is the function and health of the body's mobility, its communication within itself, its awareness to other body forms in nature, and its five physical senses. Your first and foremost function is to pay attention to your body, and once that is done, you are almost automatically put in tune with the opportunities in nature. One part of nature is the opportunity to use itself in its mothering and nurturing. This means you don't have to design what you are going to do or what happens in your life. Nature will provide it in relation to your harmony and health.

There is no *One* up above in a heavenly sense that does anything. What happens is you are in the right mode in order to utilize nature's natural action. Nature's natural action is not that much different from Universal action in that nature refuses to harm itself. It only produces the opportunity for advancement within its lifetime. No natural law intends to harm itself. Earthquakes and the mass death of animals are to balance, not to harm, and when things happen to you, the same law applies.

The Natural Key to Life

If you ask me what the natural key to life is, I would say that it is balance. It is equality in which we have the quality of harmony within the natural law. You might see that as unbelievably good fortune and experience. However, you will not be elated by that because your attitude at that point would be, "Yes, there is nothing to be elated about because this is normal." We get elated because we don't believe it is going to happen, when actually it is there all the time. You say to yourself, "Yes, but what about the moments when I feel like I have been guided? I feel like there has been some heavenly influence." You can revert back to consciousness, even for a micro-millisecond, and feel that as a great surge of universal sustenance. It has nothing to do with your problems, but you can feel that energy. The point is that when your life is not functioning the way you want it to function, it is because you are operating antagonistically to natural planetary law. The logical thing is to harmonize yourself, in receptivity, to nature and its laws. Now, you have allowed consciousness and your body to work together side-by-side without interrupting either one. You are responding and nature is responding back to you.

Before I went for my training in Tibet, I was interested in metaphysics and mind science that says the metaphysical laws are life, joy, beauty, and all of those things. However, those are not metaphysical laws at all. They are natural laws. It is not that the quality of those things is not in the Universe, but that is not metaphysical law. If we keep putting our attention at life, harmony, love, joy, peace, beauty, and abundance as metaphysical law, we are ignoring the very source. Therefore, we can't use them. The source is in the planet and in nature. If I want joy, I go to nature for my joy because consciousness already has joy. It isn't interested in passing any of it along to me because it only knows it as the wisdom of joy.

It is okay if I want joy and I come to you and you can give it, but it is wrong if I think you are the source of joy. You are not the source of it anymore than I am. The planet is the source of enjoyment, beauty, rest, entertainment, harmony, and sustenance. Those are all things that come from the planet. Therefore, you should not assign any of these as metaphysical qualities that come from heaven. That does not mean that all these qualities are not part of the Universe in a metaphysical sense, but heaven cannot provide them. The planet provides them. If I want peace, I go to the planet for peace.

Empowerment

I have delayed talking about this subject because hardly anyone wants to cope with it. However, at this particular time, you should probably take this in and do something with it. Many times I refer to the conflict between consciousness and the body. I use the word 'conflict' when, in effect, there isn't a conflict. I use the word because no one will understand when I say that consciousness is an alien inside of you. People translate that to mean conflict. In reality, it doesn't mean conflict. What you can see is your strength and your power in consciousness because you always have that, and you can always fall back on consciousness. Do it for too long and we will institutionalize you. If you do it correctly, we will see you in a minute or two (or the next day) and everything will be okay.

The fact is that the power of the planet is the power you have available to you in totality.

Part III
Family Ties

> *We are each a complete walking world.*
> *--GT*

One of the main problems of metaphysics is that it tends, by its very nature, to pull us away from a physical level and get us closer to the levels of consciousness and the metaphysical. That is okay if we are talking about minor approaches. However, the longer you stay in metaphysics and the mystical sciences, the further and further you tend to remove yourself from the planet and the body as your vehicle. Those are the very things that are tangible for you to use every single day.

It becomes necessary periodically (whatever that means in time) to go back to basics. As long as you are going to be with the planet, you cannot operate here in a metaphysical state and operate harmoniously. You cannot be removed from the planet's physical atmosphere as your current home in terms of your learning opportunities.

This is a very difficult and rare school. You are required to unify spiritual, mental, and physical energy frequencies into a single unit and work with them as a single unit. No matter how well we might do in the spiritual and mental areas, if the physical doesn't come along equally we are not going to be satisfied. We will not have a better grasp of who and what we are.

We are completely misled metaphysically when we pull away from the physical because we all chose this planet for its real and tangible nature, as much as we did for its metaphysical and occult learning lesson. As a matter of fact, it was the prime consideration to come to a place where we would establish a physical vehicle. It is the physical vehicle that houses your consciousness as a means through which to learn.

I have never been one to approve of systems that subjugate or try, in any way, to eradicate the physical body. Naturally, health is a very important issue to be considered, but more important than that is your relationship to nature and the planet. We are ruining our lakes and forests, and we don't take care of our animals. It is as if we do not have any kind of affinity with the planet or what nature is doing for us. It is very unfortunate to see such ignorance in our society. It has even come to the point that we have actually isolated ourselves from our true nature. It is true that in some respects the American Indians had a closer relationship to the planet. That is also true of almost any indigenous population, wherever we go. This is one of the reasons we find a different atmosphere in Europe. Europeans seem older by the fact that they worked the land and lived closer to their land. They have a stronger sense of their relationship to their resources. I don't have that sense in the heartland of America.

As metaphysical people, we cannot afford to abdicate our relationship to the land because, in so doing, we miss an enormous amount of our identity. We refer to Mother Nature and set Her aside as if She were some force outside of us. It is true that the laws that govern this planet, the laws of nature, are self-balancing, and it is also true that we cannot add to those laws. We can be well assured that those laws were established when the planet was established, and they are being maintained.

The main point is that we make a terrible mistake in setting nature aside as if She were a separate entity. Nature does maintain Her own balance. In reality, She is subject to the way mass consciousness operates but not subject to mass consciousness in terms of being undermined. If we do certain things to the planet to destroy lakes and forests, nature will take Her course to re-balance. She will begin to fight back. She will bring a plague or cause an earthquake. She will ignite a volcano. She will bring along a hurricane, ad infinitum. Nature will always bring Herself into self-balance. That may not be an immediate thing but, over the years, this will be done. There is a phrase that is very common at funerals: *Ashes to ashes and dust to dust.* When you are considering the physical vehicle, that phrase is very important. You borrowed your body from nature, and you are going to return it to nature.

Nature can wipe out twenty thousand, fifty thousand, one hundred thousand people at one time if you strip Her of the trees and other resources. You might look at that metaphysically, spiritually, or even humanly and say, "This is awful." I might agree with you that it is awful in that sense, but it is only what we deserve as a mass. We have taken and it must be given back.

Well Positioned

It is not as if the planet is learning. It is using a development phase. It does grow. It does reach an apex where it has completed its life. It burns itself out like any star that burns itself out. In one way or another, it will disintegrate and will no longer be here. That ending will be the ultimate balance of the planet when it has completed its sojourn. It will be replaced by a new baby planet someplace else, or in the same spot. The system goes on and on forever.

When we start talking about you metaphysically, the great requirement is the love you are to have for yourself as a physical unit of nature and the great love you are to have for nature. It must be coordinated with an affinity to you as a part of nature. This does not necessarily mean that you have to go and hug an aspen or pat an oak tree as you walk by. However, there must be some sense of affinity for the planet as an entity, as a being, and as a vitality. *You* are that vitality.

What brings us to the point of this lecture is seeing the recognition of so many people who have isolated themselves by setting the planet aside as if it were some poor relation. In its place is man who sets up his great computer and his great mind as the Master. He is not the Master. Nature does not have the same feelings as we understand human feelings, but She is saying that you are going to have to pay attention. It will get our attention in very dramatic ways.

Growth is an important factor. In this case, growth means an understanding of who you are in nature's kingdom, as well as, what you are in consciousness. At this point we must go back to the simple basics. You <u>are</u> nature and nature is you. There is no separation between you and nature. This does not diminish consciousness. It does give a proper starting point.

The human vehicle is not assigned on an astral basis. Before you incarnate, your pattern is drawn up. In other words, your blueprint is drawn up. You see that and you totally approve of it. You then decided to incarnate. The last step in that approval is your choice of parents for your genetic terminals. You are now going to choose your cells to put your body together from that family tree, that genetic line. Those cells are not assigned by heaven. The *people up upstairs* do not say, "Okay, here is the vehicle, and we are making it and shaping it." What *they* are doing and saying is, "Here is the blueprint. Here is what you are going to go and do. In reality, you must fulfill that. The requirement is yours. It is not ours. Here are the people who are going to act as your genetic terminals -- your mother and father. Now, you are going to have to work from that point of awareness."

Genetic Seeds

What happens is an interesting and exciting phenomenon. You were not shown your mother and father. You were shown types. You were shown female and male types. Those types were there because each one has had its own parent. You can quickly see how that whole line goes back and becomes enormous. That is what creates your genetic line. What actually occurs is the *Powers-that-Be* say to you, "These are the types you are going to use." You are allowed to do this just before you get into the reincarnation mode. You sit and look at the genetic family tree. The genetic line goes back to the beginning of man so we must be talking in terms of hundreds of billions of individuals. You see it as if I took you to a huge grain elevator and all the grains spilled out. There are billions and billions of grains lying there. You are told that every one of those grains has a unique quality. It is out of those qualities (based on the pattern you are going to follow) that you must pick all the grains that are to become the cells of your body. In essence, you pick tens of billions of these seeds. You see these as nature's pattern cells. You are actually picking these out of nature.

Those billions and billions and billions of tiny grain seeds are really cellular energy patterns. The concept everyone has is that you have a mother and father and that your RNA and your DNA code is all picked up from your mother and father. That is so shortsighted that it is almost sickening.

Science is working all the time to find its errors. That concept is one of its biggest errors! Your parents are simply the end terminals of this long genetic line.

What you are doing is looking back and saying, "Okay, I know what my learning lesson is, and I know I have the tools to get the job done. I know my body has to contain X number of cells in the billions." You are left alone for a period of cycles, and you go to work. Pick. Pick. Pick. It is as if there are all these tiny energy cells not yet materialized. They are not picked out of space. They are all picked from the nature of this planet. Every one of your ancestors who died left behind these little seeds. It is as if you are looking over this vast, vast farmland, and as far as your eyes can see are these seeds that are all yours. They all belong to the same pattern. You know what you want because each one is formed as an identity. You say, "Okay, from that ancestor I want this and from that ancestor I want that." You are very good at this because you have already seen your blueprint. That has already occurred.

At this particular point *the people upstairs* have, in a real sense, washed their hands of you. *They* drew up the blueprint. Once you approve it, you <u>do</u> take over. It is your responsibility to fulfill it, not *theirs*. *They* are not interested at this point about what is happening on that earth plane basis. You are. <u>You</u> are going to come. It's <u>your</u> body, and you are going to put it together. I can assure you that you are not going to sit there and say, "Oh, gee. I didn't mean to choose to be this short, or this thin, or have this nose." No, you knew exactly what you were doing. You picked every single one of them correctly. They all fit like millions of pieces of a puzzle. They all fit perfectly together, and they were all in place before you started your nine-month's period ready for an incarnation and the pregnancy of your mother.

In essence, you are part and parcel of nature. Your contact with nature and the planet started before you were even born. All of these cellular energy seeds that you picked did not come from your mother's body. This is the reason a woman goes from feeling so rotten to feeling so great during pregnancy. She has brand- new vitality seeds in her that are being fed by her system, but they are not her seeds. They are the seeds of the individual incarnating through her. In a very real sense, this is why a woman feels so elevated during pregnancy and why many women go into post pregnancy depression. Once the child has issued forth, the woman has lost all of those new seeds that were not hers anyway. She has lost all that marvelous new energy, and she is back to being herself. Sometimes she feels that being back to herself is a huge let down. The umbilical chord has been cut, and the incarnated individual is now independent.

This is really what goes on. It is nature in action. One of the things you must come to, before anything else, is how much you are a child of nature. Family ties and family relationships are all manufactured from emotional needs because there really isn't such a thing as a family the way you would like to think about family. We are *all* family. Our real mother is nature. Our real family is our natural interfacing. Certainly there is a strong affinity when you grow up in the same garden with the same people. However, we have this all misplaced because we are the children of nature first and last for that matter. Mother and father are exactly what they are intended to be. They are the genetic terminals that allowed us to make our choice off that genetic line.

We give to ourselves by our willingness to incarnate. It is nature that gives us life – the planet gives us life. If you want to get to the point of understanding family, it is really your ancestors that gave you life more than your parents. It was their seeds that they left behind that provided you choices. You are more like your ancestors than your mother and father. It is not unusual to have four or five children in a family who are all so different. Some of them don't even look like their parents.

Your allegiance and family love is to the planet that birthed you. If this were being done correctly, you would be taught very early on to recognize that the earth is your parent. A barrier is set up when you think we are much too sophisticated, and it is that barrier that has a lot to do with all your problems, your angers, your frustrations, your sense of isolation, and your psychological breakdowns. You keep trying to go to people for sustenance and support. That isn't where it is. You need to go back to nature. Nature is the very thing that birthed you.

When we are in need of something to support us, we turn to things like water. What keeps you well? It is the herbs, plants, and food of nature. The air is what keeps you alive. You drew all of your cells from nature. Every time you ignore that, every time you look with expectation to another human to give you that sustenance, you set yourself apart from the very thing that gave you life. You cannot afford to do that and still be the kind of person who you want to be.

In Control

There is a point at birth that is unbelievably amazing. It makes one realize the intricacy of the Universe. It is true that after you made your genetic choice, you are who you are. You are that child of nature. There is an interesting phenomenon that takes place. Consciousness does not belong to this planet. Consciousness belongs to the Universe. That is its Source. Now, consciousness is required to move in and take control of this physical vehicle. All those seed cells that are yours were being nurtured by your mother during her pregnancy. All of sudden those seed cells are all issued forth into a physical vehicle which is no longer being sustained by the mother. Consciousness takes over.

Consciousness must impress every cell with the total blueprint and pattern. At the same time it does that, it harmonizes the physical vehicle and keeps it within the perimeters of understanding nature as its source. This is a *marvelous* thing that takes place. All of a sudden the body (truly the body of nature) now becomes the body that also stores the consciousness. There occurs an attitude in which the body now recognizes itself as an individual – which it does the moment of first breath – and also recognizes that it has consciousness as its domain. Nevertheless, its relationship to nature is fidelity and protection to Nature -- the very Mother who birthed it. Nature gives you your life. The minute you have it under the control of consciousness, you owe it to Nature to protect Her. That is the planetary law. The recognition is that your first action, your first commitment is to the protection of the planet.

We don't do that. We simply know we must protect our land, and we know that is where our fidelity should go. However, we are not taught from Day One that fighting to possess the land is a destructive misconception of what protection truly means. Every war is about the protection of land. You know how people go about protecting their land, whether you are talking about their front yard or protecting their country. That comes about as a misconception about our job as to how we protect our birthright, our power, our planet, and our energy. We have it all misconstrued. From Day One, you must learn to take care of those plants that sustain your life. You must take care of the planet that birthed you. It is no less than your own physical body. It is everything to you, and you must never turn your back on it, desert it, or destroy it. You give to it what it needs. That is taking dominion.

Little children know this. They get along with the flowers and are fascinated with the little animals and the bugs. They sit in trees. That is what tree houses are all about! Before it is taught out of them, they recognize that nature is their home. They have a right to live in it. Nature is their family. The human attitude has lost this understanding of dominion. John Donne said, "No man is an island." Something goes out of our family when a tree dies. It is also true that when you die, we lose you. However, we don't lose you so much as a human being, but we lose that part of nature that you represented. It is sad in one way, but the happiness is that nature will re-generate from that and give us another child, another person, another thing.

I might also point out to you that there is the Indian concept that you die and come back as animals. We don't come back as animals, but the concept came from the understanding that nature recycles itself. It is the elements of your body (not your consciousness) that are recycled through nature. Animal nature is part of the planetary unit and is used as another animal. As nature makes its changes, species will die out and new ones will come about. It has been a number of years since we have had dinosaurs because that is the growth to where we are. Let them go. That is how nature goes through its cycles as a pool of consciousness but not through individualized consciousness. It is humans who have individualized consciousness that enters the physical vehicle at the time of birth. Up to that point, the body is a vehicle that belongs to nature and is nurtured by the human mother.

By Design

You didn't just happen. You are not here accidentally. You

are actually designed by a blueprint that was set up in consciousness before you incarnated. I can assure you that generally the way you look today is the way you have allowed yourself to become or forced yourself to become, and I can tell you, unequivocally, that there has never been and never will be a person who is designed for this planet who is not beautiful. If you could show me an ugly plant, I would back down. You can't. *Everything* in nature always has some aspect that is beautiful and outstanding.

There are people who are made ugly by their attitudes, but they are beautiful by design. You can have a garden full of peonies and a garden full of asters, and no two are the same. They are all beautiful. What is naturally missing is that a person moves away from the original design when moving away from nature. The tendency is to not understand your original fascination with nature. You do not stop to recognize that when you have an affinity to a tree it is because, in your nature, you are very much like that tree in terms of design. The same thing is true with your affinity to an animal. This is why some people are crazy about boxers and large dogs and some people like small lapdogs. All those designs of nature are within you. You have that affinity for your nature.

Your design within nature was done in order to allow you to accomplish very definitive tasks in very definitive ways. This insistence that we look alike, act alike, and harmonize is just too irrational. We desperately lose sight of our individuality and our uniqueness. It is a violation of nature more than it is a violation of consciousness. You are YOU. Any effort on your part to make yourself the same as someone else (or to feel you must be like others) puts you in an awful, awful situation! It's like saying to an aspen that it can no longer be an aspen. It must now be a scotch pine. That is so utterly ridiculous that you wouldn't even consider it.

However, that is no more ridiculous than you insisting that you must be like another person or that another person must be more like someone else. Putting children together in a group and telling them they must all do something all alike and at the same time amounts to the same thing.

There is a lot being said these days about doing things for the good of the *team* in the workplace. There is no such thing as *teamwork* without individuals. The only thing that makes a person a good team member is that he knows himself as an individual. Individuals know how to harmonize with those things around themselves, in this case, the team. It is because the tree knows it's a tree that makes it work well in the forest. If it didn't, it wouldn't! Never think that a person gives up identity to become a good team worker. What makes him good is individual identity that sometimes means he keeps his mouth shut because he knows he is good. That is why he can get along and be a good team player. If you have a whole team of those people, they are unstoppable.

There need be no question in your mind as to the one design that gets you to fulfill the learning experiences. You are learning in your own way using the tools you have. No one else is expressing what you are learning in your way. You and your design are one-of-a-kind. You are doing you. That is why it is *essential* to be aware of who and what you are. Without that, you do not know who, what, or where you are, nor do you know what direction to go. You might wait around for someone to tell you. In that case, you are following the Pied Piper right down to the end of the road.

Humanoids

Humanoids are types. They are the types in the same way

that plants, trees and animals are types. You can't modify a type. You can sophisticate it. What does that mean? It means that you can't change a horse from being a horse, but you can go from a wild horse, to a plow horse, to a sleek racehorse. Humans don't go through modifications. We go through levels of sophistication. You become better, but you don't change. You take what you basically are (and that is infinite progression), and you sophisticate it. You take your beauty and you become more beautiful. That is not a change of looks. That is a sophistication of looks. You are human. You stay human. You have two eyes and a mouth. You have a torso, two legs, and two arms. You have male parts if you are male and female parts if you are female.

If you want to go back to Darwinian concepts, that is still humanoids. Although, something has been missed in the theory of creation. Humans have always been humans and always will be humans. Nothing is going to change that. We are different than our parents and much different than our forefathers. We are taller and stronger in many ways. We have different brain capacities. There are a lot of things that we are that they weren't. As we look one hundred to two hundred years down the road, we might go into other sophistications. It is true that the less we use our bodies, the less powerful the body will be built, but it is still the basic body parts with different sophistication.

I think this is the real beauty of human types in nature. It is like looking at some of those marvelous old oaks that are a couple of hundred years old. What do you see? It's like a matriarch who has found her place among the family and has taken her stately position. We are the microcosm to the planetary macrocosm. We are (for ourselves) the small microcosm to nature's world. Within every one of us are the trees, the animals, the water, and the air. We are the very things that the planet is. We walk around as self-contained planetary units, and that is why we drink water and eat food. We are not just replenishing our bodies. We are replenishing the microcosmic unit, which is a carbon copy of the macrocosmic planet. This is why we love certain weather and why it refreshes some people when it rains and depresses others. Why would this happen if you were not part of nature? Animals go off and hide, or they get angry, and they act in certain ways as a result of being affected by the atmosphere. We do exactly the same thing. A sunny day can uplift you and make you feel warm. It can make you want to curl up and just bask in the warmth of the sun like a snake feeling the warmth of a rock.

You really do hang onto every single aspect of the wider world of nature. This is why you are nomadic and absorb the world. It is like taking your world and refurbishing it, by reflection, to other parts of the world. The knowledge of who you are provides you a vital framework that allows you to harmonize with your surroundings. To *feel* this you need the identification of who and what you are. The closer you are to that identification, the more empathy you have and the more comfortable you are with that tree, and that plant, and that animal because you know that you are that species. This gives you not only joy, but it also gives you vital sustenance. You refurbish by knowing what you are within the concept of that tree and that plant. A herbologist might tell you that in order to feel better you need to eat a certain herb. That is telling you that you are that plant. This is how you use food to learn who and what you are. You cannot separate yourself from nature without damaging your over-all capacity.

How you see yourself is not a point for us to argue. However, if it differs from the way others see you in the nature kingdom, you are not transmitting the natural characteristics out of nature. When that becomes evident to you, your association with nature needs your attention. Visit the zoo and wild animal parks. Go into nature to get a better *feeling* for the species you have identified with to see what they are like. The more you know about that species, the more you will express that part of your nature. Otherwise, a lack of communication within your natural expression hampers every interface you have with other people, and they see you as different types of nature than you see yourself. Therefore, they treat you the way they see you, not the way you see yourself. They do not treat you the way you expect to be treated. They do not talk to you the way you expect to be talked to, nor do they handle you the way you expect to be handled. How, then, can you go through life feeling that you have good relationships? You can't. Blocks occur that are much more than psychological. I am walking through the woods. I see you as a pussycat, but you identify yourself as a cougar. We are going to be in a lot of trouble getting along!

A State of Refinement

How you see yourself as all of these elements put together in one physical vehicle in this particular atmosphere is a state of refinement. The following are some categories that I highly recommend you use to clarify what you are transmitting. Quickly identify the species you have an affinity for within each category. I assure you, you *can truly believe* what first occurs to you.

- A tree.
- A plant.
- A flower.
- A bird.
- A fish.
- An animal.
- A type of mineral.

Your cells belong to the planet, and they know everything they need to know about the planet. You can seek your point of refinement as you refine yourself upward, just as a little sapling grows and fills itself out. It becomes itself and establishes its refinement. You can do exactly the same thing. You have probably never looked at yourself as a physical body through which everything passes as a molecule of crystalline, bird, fish, flower, tree, or air. You are an unusual and multi-faceted animal.

See the Appendix <u>after</u> you make your identifications. There you will find a reference to the meaning of relationships within each category. In order for you to receive the full benefit from your cellular storage unit, it is essential for you to make your identifications <u>before</u> accessing the Appendix, or you will not have a first time awareness that can only happen once.

Conclusion
Terrestrial Activities

> *The essence in talking about consciousness has a great deal to do with where you are going.*
> --GT

We are going to start out with a quasi-quiz, which is not really a quiz, but I need you to write down the answers to ten questions before we begin. These will hopefully give you a point of reference as we progress. It is a fill-in-the-blank type of questionnaire:

1. I will reach my most important life goal in _____ (number of) years.
2. When my net income reaches _____ dollars, I will be wealthy.
3. The perfect partner for me is _____ years old, _____ feet tall, weighs _____, and is in _____ career.
4. The food my body could best exist on, if it were the only food available is_____.
5. The place on the planet where I would be most happy is _____.
6. I would be most satisfied with ____ number of friends.
7. The ideal number of hours for me to work each day is _____.
8. I would pay _____ dollars for a diamond ring.
9. My ideal color is _____.
10. If I could attain to any public office, it would be_____.

Now, please put all of this aside, and we will return to these questions in due course.

****

Where *are* you going? What *are* you doing? What are the results going to be? We live in a system that does not promote individuality. We do live in a system that promotes everyone doing the same thing with everyone going in the same direction at the same time. We are to eat three meals a day within certain given hours, and none of this promotes individual living. What if you are not hungry? You are force fed, and your digestive system doesn't distribute the food as fuel to be put to good use.

Consequently from day one, you tend to begin to design your life on what the masses do or what the system says. This is particularly true when you start off to school. School is one of the most regimented experiences in life, probably even more so than military life. Bells ring at a certain time. You must have a certain number of books, a certain number of teachers, and necessary passing grades, ad infinitum. The fact that all this regimentation comes so early in life leaves a lasting effect. You start out roughly at the age of five years, and you are not out of it until around age eighteen. It becomes very, very difficult to break out of that pattern. You are looking at thirteen years of intensive regimentation and, by then, any sense of individuality has been wiped out in terms of breaking out of the system. Certainly there are some diversions you are willing to take but, as a rule, nothing very dramatic. When the bell goes off, you will do what you are supposed to do – more or less – with little variation.

For those of you who come into metaphysics, you hear a great deal about 'doing your own thing'. Everything in metaphysics is pointed toward bringing you into your own individuality. We can give a lot of lip service to independence and individuality. Nevertheless, 'doing your own thing' is very, very hard to do. By the time you are ready to take on whatever is to be done, you have no idea what it is you want to do. You have a very difficult time in striking out to do the things that are good for you and to do them in the way that is good for you because you are already locked into the system. The idea of turning around and becoming something else or 'doing your own thing' is not easy.

The consistent response I get from almost everyone I talk to when we get into this subject is, "I don't know what I want to do. I can't figure out what is the right direction. I can't figure out what is good for me." That is true because we don't inventory ourselves. When we do, it is only partially done. We are never trained to know our upper and lower limits. We need those limits in order to find a mid-point.

If you go back to school, you hear a lot about excelling, "Well, you could do better. You are a C student, but you really could be an A student." You really don't know what that means. Or, if you go out and play a sport, you are told you could do much better. That is a competitive comment. You don't know what that means because you are not competitive.

The Universe is not competitive. Competition does not exist in the Universe. Things in nature do not compete with each other. They just follow their plan. You will never get anywhere in life if you are going to compete against anybody else, and you will get far less in life if you start competing with yourself. It is lip service if you look at this from the standpoint of reaching out as if you can do better. What does it mean to do better when you think you are doing as well as you can? What does it mean to go in a different direction when you are pretty well convinced that the direction you are going in is the direction you should be going? Or maybe you have convinced yourself that you don't know any other direction to go.

What I am getting at is that you get to a point in life when you wake up and realize that the essence of metaphysics is individualistic. Then what? You don't have any foundation to know how to deal with events in terms of who you are, what you are, and where you need to go. Without that you don't have any basis for an evaluation to anchor yourself. It makes little difference if this occurs in your 30's, 40's, 50's or much later.

You need to understand that the very basis of life is individual direction. You don't get any gold stars when you are finished with this lifetime in terms of what you have *done* for other people unless you were sent to be a Messiah. You weren't sent to do anything for anybody else. You were sent with a singular learning lesson and specific directions for the purpose of your own individual growth. Heaven knows, how many times I hear in any given day, "Well, I do this for so-n-so, and this for kids, and this for my parents" – whatever the case may be. Thinking that in some way that should provide an entry into heaven. That isn't going to happen! I am guaranteeing my soul on it. That is not going to happen. There is nobody at the pearly gates keeping book on you. When it is all over with here, you are going to run your own balance sheet. All those things you said you did *for* and *gave to* other people are going to amount to zero. If there was a voice to greet you when you pass over, the question would be: What did you do as it pertains to your growth and development?

There are attitudes within the system that say that is it selfish to do for oneself. That attitude takes away from individuality. We live in a society that says that you *must* help your neighbor. That is considered a good Christian thing to do. So, you are busy helping your neighbor, and who is busy helping you? Your junk is piling up at your doorstep while you are busily sweeping off your neighbors doorstep and taking care of someone else. You do not walk in their shoes. How do you <u>know</u> you are helping?

To this very day, I claim that I really don't help people. There is no way I could help them because I don't walk in their shoes. I don't have their background. I can say things, but I am saying these for me, not for you. I can't help you. You can help you. We make major efforts, certainly in vain, to make input to other people's lives. We *think* we are making their lives better, but we don't know we are making their lives any better. We are certainly not making our lives better if we are fooling ourselves into thinking that by making a contribution we have somehow become better people.

Metaphysics goes back to a very honest basis that no one wants to look at. All the things that you are going to do for others, you cannot do unless you do them for yourself. You cannot love, unless you love you. You can't give joy, unless you're joyful. You can't give wisdom, unless you are wise. You can't give comfort, unless you are peaceful. You can't give good advice, unless you yourself are abundant. All these things that we are so willing to give away, we don't have. Sometimes we like to think we have them, but we don't have them. If we did have them, we wouldn't have to give them away. They would just radiate out.

A candle does not give its flame away to the dark. It just burns. It radiates. The dark falls back where the flame is, and there is no more darkness. The flame did not give anything to the dark. It is just the flame. A human being fulfilling all the prime requirements for its individuality does exactly the same thing. You don't have to give anything. You walk down the street and everybody says, "Oh, terrific. I don't know what she's got, but it's terrific" and you did it without giving it. That is really the essence.

You Are Here

The point is you are here, and you wouldn't be here for any other good reason than your own development. It is no mistake you are in this society. It means that somewhere along the line you are going to have to learn how to change. The basis for this is the recognition that this is your life. No one can contribute to it, and no can take away from it. You really are in control. The whole object of the ten questions is to try to get you to see some of the values of how those controls are put into effect. Every time I bring this subject up, people usually fall back and say, "Oh, you are really talking rebellion. To do this I have to leave family and friends and go off and be something of an independent rebel." <u>That is not true at all</u>. Life increases in quality when you become individualistic. It does not diminish.

You will lose friends who were not friends to begin with. You will gain new associations far better than the ones you lost. More than anything, the degree of awareness you have in terms of power and control of your own life exceeds anything you could buy, beg, or steal under the present conditions of society. The problem is that you never know that until you do it. It's one of those things that I could talk about forever. It is like reincarnation. You never know until you do it!

This business of individuality will never become a reality to *you* until one day you wake up and say, "You know, I've really done this, it does work, and it is pleasant and fulfilling." The biggest argument comes in relationships because people don't understand how you can have individuality between individuals. Individuality builds respect and respect is what relationships are built upon. Love is a word that is as undefined as any word I know. If I value me, I value the other person. If the other person values herself or himself, as the case may be, then they value me. I would not do to the other person what I would not do to myself. That sounds a little bit like something out of *The Bible* that has come to be known as the Golden Rule: *Do unto others as you would have them do unto you.* It's true! If I think well of me, I wouldn't do something that is unwell to the other person. That is degradation to me.

Therefore, a relationship is built upon my quality and another person's quality working harmoniously to enjoy both qualities. At that point the qualities run parallel. Giving or taking in a relationship doesn't really exist. That is part of the fallacy. Because when you give to or take from a relationship, there goes the individuality. When individuality goes, there goes the relationship. Sooner or later, all you are doing is keeping book. *You did this for me so I will do this for you* is not a relationship. It has to be a sense of doing for yourself and that encompasses a lot of events around you, which encompass a lot of people around you.

You don't go out and push the darkness back. You glow, and the darkness pulls back. If you are good as individuals, everybody close to you benefits and responds to that. They use that as they see fit, and you are very happy in letting them use it because you didn't really *give*. It was just you being you.

Direction

It becomes a value in life to have an identification of individual direction. That will never stay the same because changes occur event to event. Although I like to talk in terms of the ultimate, there are bad days. My panacea for that is to stay in bed, pull the covers over your head, and forget it. Tomorrow, start all over again. The idea to go around and think you are going to change the world when you are having a bad day is ridiculous. You are just having a bad day. You made a mistake. So what? That is not the end of the world. What you have got to understand is that, for the most part, you are focusing and trying. That is all that really counts. You are not, by any stretch of the imagination, supposed to be a saint. You show me anybody who makes a grand effort to focus and give only to other people, and I will show you a person who is a bell without a clapper. Their life is practically worthless. They try to build their life on the basis of other people's response to them, and that is how they live. They haven't got much in the way of their life. The bell is there. The clapper isn't.

Part of reaching individuality and independence is the ability to grow up and become mature. Maturity is an enormously important element in metaphysics. The change from where you are non-metaphysically to metaphysically is a matter of maturity. Stop being a little girl and a little boy and grow up. Take responsibility and realize that this is totally your life from beginning to end. You do it – fine. You don't do it – who the hell cares? Nobody cares, but in the end result you are going to run the balance sheet and realize you haven't done anything. You haven't realized any results from this thing called life.

Maturity is recognizing those things that you have to do that you don't always want to do. Speaking when you need to speak, or holding your tongue when you know it is the wise thing to do. Recognize the need to correct yourself because you are acting like a spoiled child and take on responsibility. Realize that your main issue is to carry your own load. Once you get onto that, your life can change dramatically. Happiness becomes a commonplace thing in your life beyond what you have yet to experience.

We have other elements that really dominate and cause interference with the individual life other than what we have covered so far. Recognizing that the system becomes a catchall and provides the framework, we then have elements within the system that definitely turn out to be the bogeyman. I want to touch upon those because those elements are all on the material, physical level.

Elements of Interference

1. Fear: The first point of interference is fear. Fear, like love, is impossible to define. Fear is individualistic. It is everything from fear of the future, to fear of the boss, to fear of poverty, to whatever is identified by an individual. Fear is taught to us from day one in the human sense. Everything that resides in society to provide some limit represents some kind of fear. It can be anything. Don't pay your bills and there is the fear of being sued. Don't earn a living, and there is a fear of starving and being destitute. Don't take care of your health and there is fear of illness. Don't do this and there is fear of that. Fear becomes a tool through which society controls its people. Something is being threatened, and it is usually harm. We are convinced from day one that we can be harmed. That starts out as a little child when you put your hand on something hot, and the parents jump and say, "Don't! That will burn you. Don't cross the street. You could get run down." The fear is established even before the event could happen.

In the first five years, you are fear oriented. The limitations put on by parents are the lower limitations of what society has put upon them. By the time you are five or six years old you are saying, "I can't do this because of _____"(you can fill in the blank because of some kind of fear that has been instilled into you). There is a fear of embarrassment that comes from the fear of what people will think about you. You are afraid of being laughed at, rejected, or pointed out as different. We really build a catalogue of fears in those first five years. Generally, eighty to eighty-five percent of fears are the same for all of us. The other fifteen percent are individualistic, depending on how we were raised. There are different fears that fit our particular growth and make-up patterns, but we all end up basically living in fear.

You can't find individuality within fear because it is the system's way of making you dependent on the system. The system is saying, "Look, we are in a lot of trouble here, and you have got to do this right. If you do it right, we will protect you. If you do it wrong, you are in trouble." What do you do? You tend to embrace the system, and the system says, "Yes, that is good, and you are a good child. Now come in and keep doing it right. We won't have any trouble at all. Show up every morning at 9:00, and you won't have any trouble." You think, "Well, that is the way of staying out of trouble." Everybody shows up at 9:00 and everybody goes to lunch at noon and everybody goes home at 5:00. Now you are safe, so you say. What happens if the system wants to change from 9:00 to 10:00? All of a sudden you have to change, or else.

2. <u>Greed</u>: The second point of interference is greed. I think I can tolerate almost anything in a human being except greed, although it is present in every phase of our society. In fact, it is practically the impetus that runs the whole business community in one way or another. Greed is a broad word like fear encompassing a lot of things. It is *I get mine* but not necessarily before you get yours. It is just that *I get mine and then some*. In other words, we never get to a point of what is enough because we don't know what enough is. Using the laws of the jungle, we look around and everybody is taking a bite so we better take two bites. Everyone has a

handful. We better take two handfuls. The system is built upon *you better save your money.* Saving your money is greed. That is taking money that you could use and put into action, but you can't do that because everyone is saying that you better save your money, or you will lose it. The bank says that it will save it for you. While they are saving it for you, they are making about twenty-two percent on it, and sometimes they will give you five or six percent while they take the rest. That is greedy. A reasonable share would be for them to take eleven percent and give you eleven persent. Instead, they keep sixteen percent. That is greed. Meanwhile, you hold onto money accumulating more and more, which is also greed.

The system works all the way up to the top and all the way to the bottom. If you look behind every phase of crime, you will find some sort of greed as it applies to power as greed. As long as greed is there, it will undermine individuality because you are not thinking "I" in a metaphysical sense. You are thinking "I" in a competitive sense. I have to get it for me. The rule then becomes: Do unto others before they do unto you. Get what you can before someone takes it away from you. This works in ways that simply escape you because greed can be so insidious. Stop and ask yourself: Do I really need this? The question is not the need if you have eighteen items in your wardrobe. The question is: Do you <u>use</u> eighteen items in your wardrobe? It isn't greedy if you use the items. It is greedy if you don't use them. If you use three homes, it isn't greed. If you don't use them, it is greed.

Greed puts all of us in a position of under-mining the very system that we are using to prosper because it promotes the excess and the holding of excesses. In effect, the excess is in the hands of the few, and what is left for the rest is very little. That increases the amount of greed in those who don't have because they don't have a decent share. Mind you, I am also assuming they are working and making an effort, not just sitting back waiting for a handout. This causes the very imbalance in society that is detrimental.

We shouldn't have any welfare in a country this size with such abundance. There is plenty to do and there is plenty to share. I am not talking in a communistic sense. Because of greed, all the power and wealth is held by the few. The rest are left to fight for it. In the fighting for it, there is more intensity in the area of greed in order to get more and more. The system becomes defeated because it does not share, and therefore it does not grow and develop. Greed now becomes an element of fear, and fear is the first item on the list that holds individuality away from us.

3. <u>Confusion:</u> The third point of interference is confusion. Again, confusion is one of these catchall words. Confusion is that state in which we recognize we are not in control. In effect, we are not in a position in our own life to move in the way that we so choose. In talking with people about their own subject matter, what it really comes down to is this statement: *I don't know. I don't know what I want. I don't know what direction I want to go.* It isn't that they don't know. It is just that they are confused. People are confused. We can't possibly grow up in this society being reasonably aware without being totally confused.

There is a ratio. The more aware you become, the more confused you become because there are so many conflicting elements. Look at the area of health alone. Chinese acupuncturists say this and nutritionists say that. One faction says you will never recover from cancer, and another faction says you will never recover from a certain type of cancer. Yet another faction says you can recover from any kind of cancer. Who are you going to believe? Whomever you want to believe, but even that is an entrée into confusion because you are never sure that you are sure. Every time you think you have a fact in your life that straightens out confusion, another fact develops and you are confused again. You can't believe anything because you can't find a commonality.

If I were dictator in this country, I would pass a law that no one could advertise that they were the best unless they were judged the best by a jury. Everyone who advertised they had the best hamburger without having been judged by a Hamburger Jury would go to jail. Anyone who advertised *this was the biggest sale ever* would go to jail unless a judge determined this was the biggest sale ever seen. This promotes a state of confusion among everyone. People become immune to the meaning of words. When you open a paper and see "The Seasons Most Gigantic Sale" and turn the page to "The Seasons Most Gigantic Value," then, all of a sudden, everything is gigantic. If you are really serious about going out shopping, you wonder which gigantic you should use. It becomes very confusing as to who sells for less. When you talk to these people, they tell you it is part of the game of free enterprise. This perpetuates and contributes to the state of confusion.

I come along in a metaphysical way and say, "Why don't you make up your own mind? Why don't you find your own center point as you go along?" You say that you would like to, but that every time you get out there with friends and family, television and radio (and heaven knows what) everybody is giving you another piece of advice about what to do and how to do it. You don't know what to do. One of the things individuality demands is that you make up your own mind by experience.

Laziness goes along with confusion. We tend to be so ungodly lazy! This is an issue of maturity, as in responsibility. "I don't want to have to go out and evaluate this." Take something like buying a car: "I want a car, but I don't know which one I want." You go to showrooms and are hyped by each salesperson to buy their car. You come away realizing it is a lot of work trying to buy a car and trying to get the best deal for how much money you have to spend. If you don't want a car, try buying a computer. That will drive you crazy in no time at all. There is very little standardization so there is confusion all the time. It becomes a jungle. You have to put the confusion aside. You have to put out a tremendous effort, not so much about whether it is good or bad, but rather what is *good for you*. Metaphysically you can't eliminate confusion by just sitting on your laurels.

4. <u>Dominance:</u> The fourth point of interference with your individuality is dominance. This is actually a framework for the other three. Dominance (in any form) usually started out with parents that dominated your lifestyle, your education, and your methodology of doing things. We do live in a society made up of laws and rules. People say that without law and order humanity would run chaotically. I disagree with that totally. However, society would have to be replaced by another system. Replaced metaphysically, everyone would be taught from day one what individuality is and the quality of that individuality. I am not saying there wouldn't be a bad apple in the barrel. I <u>am</u> saying we would not be running chaotically. Domination, like anything else, is a whole way of life. It is somewhat like the game King of the Hill. Today someone is King of the Hill but, sooner or later, someone knocks him off the hill. That doesn't knock the hill down. That just knocks him off and someone else takes his place. The whole system dominates that way.

If you are going to have consciousness move you into your own space, you need a realization that you are unwilling to be dominated by individuals in the system. You will just not allow it. That does not mean you will not cooperate. In fact,

I don't think an uncooperative attitude is individualistic. It is a point of stupidity. It's like spitting in the wind. I don't think that is intelligence. I think individualistic is recognizing that you are not going to waste any energy in undermining or blowing up the system. You are just going to understand the game and what the system is. You put yourself in the position that you are not going to be dominated by it, and you are not going to fight it. You are not going to waste that kind of energy. You leave the system alone and let it do its thing. Remember the dragon only breathes fire out its nose. That means you sit on its tail and you are not going to get burned. It's still a dragon, but you are not going to get burned. You understand the system has built-in weakness. Go sit on its tail and it won't even know you are there.

<u>Fear, greed, confusion and dominance are the four monsters you will not entertain</u>. To whatever degree you can minimize these, your self-determination will give you your center point for your direction in life about what is good for you. Consciousness knows, in its own way, that you are unwilling to accept these four monsters and gives you some support and some direction. We are just going to speed up the process with awareness.

Instead of getting up in the morning and feeling that you are subject to fate or to conditions you don't like in a negative sense, realize that you are looking at a blank canvas with a whole handful of paint brushes in your hand There are also pots of paints, and you can pretty well paint your own picture. You can't learn unless you are presented with a series of events – opportunities. The event is there because that is the way life presented it to you, but it is presented as a blank canvas, an opportunity. It is up to you to decide, by virtue of free will, how you are going to handle that event, or what part of that event will benefit you the most.

Social Security

If there is anything you don't want in life, it is to plateau out. You want life to be challenging. You want it to give you all sorts of elements, which allow you to use yourself in a variety of ways. I know that you would sometimes like to say that you are tired and would just like to stop for a minute. Everyone feels that way, but the other part of that point is that we really don't have much time. You figure that, by averages, you are going to stick around eighty-five years. Twenty-odd years are used up learning how to tie your shoes. That leaves you sixty-some years with another good ten years of that time bouncing off the walls. Thirty years are gone before you turn around. How easy it is to avoid these events and waste another thirty years. Even two years is a shame to waste. You don't need rest time. You just need balancing time to restore the body. You definitely don't need to sit there and say, "Well, I don't want to do this, or I need this and I need that before I can do anything productive."

Some serious point of recognition of what you want out of life is one of the first elements that helps you. What is the statement in granite over the State House in Sacramento? *Send me men to match my mountains.* I bring this up because that is a great motto for an individual to live by. *Send me challenges to match my creativity.* After all, that is what we are here for. Wouldn't it be terrible in life if I gave you just the things you wanted within the limitations you put on what you wanted? My God, it would be awful. You would never go, never reach, never learn; and, worst of all, you wouldn't have the joy and experience that would come from the satisfaction of doing. You never would. You would be very much like the animals in the jungle that just concern themselves with survival. Eat. Sleep. Procreate. That is why they are animals. Humans have the opportunities to move within events and gain something from them. Therefore, it is essential you welcome the challenges beyond the issue of survival.

Magnetic Attraction

Events don't get there because of what we do. You can give me an argument in which you say, "Well, didn't today come about because of yesterday, and will not tomorrow be what it is because of today?" The answer is that, by-and-large, this is true because everything is continuity. That is true. An extension of your background experience occurs the moment that you are born into this lifetime in terms of the learning lesson. If you keep tracing it back, the extension does not go back to any single thing. The line is infinite. This is a hard argument to conclude either pro or con. The point is that events that are produced by the conglomerate action of life itself are attracted by you for your purposes. Simply put, nothing is given to you in life, by the way of an event, that you did not ask for. That is the truth. Nothing happens that you didn't ask for. Oh God, does that not set up arguments. The first thing you think of is all the so-called bad things that happen in your life. You say, "I didn't ask for them. No one would ask for those things to happen." You have to understand metaphysically what this means.

Somewhere in your make-up you consciously expected that self-fulfilling prophecy. As part of your learning experience, you maneuvered it and asked for it to be there so that you could have the opportunity to learn by it, to produce by it, or to gain by it no matter how terrible you considered it to be. <u>Do not</u> get yourself concerned about somebody else's pattern. I don't care how much we may like or love each other, if I find out tonight that you have died, that has *nothing* to do with me. That isn't something that I attracted.

That is in *your* pattern. The fact that I am aware of it is not that I *attracted* that. I did not *attract* your death. I am aware of it, but I am aware of people dying all over this globe at any given time. What we must understand is not to insert somebody's life pattern into our own experience. What you do is what you do. If I find that you have gone out and murdered somebody and that you are in jail, it is not for me to wonder why it is in my life. It is not in my life. It is in your life. If I want to do something about it, that is my choice. You *really* have to be clear about this! I think one of the really terrible elements in life is people getting wrapped up in being so convinced that something is their karmic debt and their cross to bear. I find this particularly true in close relationships.

It is not a truism, as a lot of people would have you believe, that as you progress in metaphysics none of these things occur in your life. There are always incidents in your life that you look at and say, "I am sorry to see that happen." You learn that it is either there because you drew it in and it becomes an event in your life, or the incident is on someone else's pattern. You may be sorry for them because you would not want to have to deal with it yourself, or you can understand how difficult it is for them. However, it is *their* pattern. This teaches you your independence. Your pattern is your pattern.

We must stop lying to ourselves. The closest person to you (or whoever has been close to you) is really hurting for some reason. Can you really feel total empathy for that person? No, you cannot because you are not walking in their shoes. You can transfer their experience to a like experience of yours to know how *it* hurts, but you don't know how *they* hurt. You just know how the experience hurts. You can't know how they hurt. You don't live inside of them. You don't have their background. This is part of growing up and learning. You have got to embrace events. *Send me men to match my mountains.* ***Send me events to match my great creativity, my great intelligence, and my great responsibility so that I can grow.*** You must allow yourself to come to that realization.

What the Universe does for us (what Life does for us) is put together a very complex pattern of molecules on our behalf for the event we are asking for. We have a bad habit of saying that we do not want what shows up for us. When we keep doing that, we get into a situation very much like the boy who called, "Wolf!" Do you know what happens when we keep asking and rejecting, asking and rejecting, asking and rejecting? Life eventually says, "To hell with it. *We* are not going to give you anymore." If you keep throwing it away, life is not going to go to all the trouble of making these complex opportunities for you, and so it doesn't. You then see that as a boring life. You say, "Nothing is happening to me."

People say to me in the counseling room that they are bored. Right away the bells go off in my head. They wouldn't be so bored if they didn't throw away everything they had. They had all these opportunities and now Life says *"We are not going to do this anymore."* What you then get isn't interesting, and life appears to be boring. There again, you made that choice. You have to understand that the Universe is always going to provide something that you can use. Even those things that you consider 'bad' and decide you truly don't want need to be questioned. How did you get it? I couldn't have gotten it if you didn't ask for it so how did you ask for it? Nine times out of ten, I can tell you how you asked for it. You believed it. It is a self-fulfilling prophecy. "I <u>know</u> I am not going to have the money when that bill comes." The bill comes in and you don't have the money. That's right. "I <u>know</u> I am going to get this cold. Everybody around me is getting a cold." You come down with a cold. If you are seriously honest with yourself, you will find that ninety- nine percent of the things that occur in your life that you don't want is self-fulfilling prophecy. What you have done is tell the Universe that you want to suffer. The Universe, on behalf of your learning experience, is happy to oblige.

You need (and truly want) to recognize that the event in your life is your proving ground. It is your fertile ground. It's your garden. If you don't have that, you don't have any place to plant, and you don't have anything to plant. You want the event. You don't want the event in negativity, but you don't have to have it in negativity. You absolutely do want it as a challenge. Absolutely! You want the challenge because you want to reach. That is how you grow and develop a little bit beyond the tip of your fingers, a little bit beyond a sense of love and awareness, and a little bit beyond the joy you have had. Yes, you want to reach. You want to extend the mountain. The Universe is intelligent, and It is not going to put an event in there that is beyond your grasp, a little bit in front of your reach, but not beyond your grasp.

The first rule of the continuity for living is you can reach for anything and eventually get it. You are actually looking at life and saying, "This is what I want." The question can come up, now, about how long should an event last? How long does it have to be there in order for you to gain some momentum? How long does it take you to learn? How long does it take you to gain from this event out of your storehouse of creative knowledge in order to go on? I don't know that for you. Sometimes relationships have to go on for fifty years before you find out you made a mistake, sometimes five minutes. Sometimes you have to go through poverty most of your life to realize you didn't have to go through poverty. Sometimes you never learn. I don't know how long that goes on. That fits into the category of what *you* think. In reality, if you have a situation in which you say, "Okay, I am having an event that has elements that I truly don't want" then you have the power to grow up enough to see what you did to bring in the event. Again, it is self-fulfilling prophecy. It's in your thinking mechanism. Okay, then you are going to have to change that.

Going around boo-hooing and expecting somebody else to give you strokes and somebody else to change it for you is an exercise in futility. Why do that? It isn't their job to do that. Somehow, people have the idea that maturity means a lack of fun. That is simply not true! It isn't less; it's more. When I look back on my life from where I started, I think I have grown up a lot. It has been more fun, not less fun, all the time. When I was immature, I was miserable. Now that I think I am grown up and taking the responsibility, I am having a lot more fun.

The importance is that the event is yours unless you deem it inappropriate to accept it as part of your life. Then, you simply figure it out. Otherwise, life will appear boring and there will be no growth factors for you. You don't have to prognosticate and be a crystal gazer. You just get up in the morning and say, "This is going to be terrific." Change your thinking right away every time your mind starts thinking of the limitation or of the things you don't want. If that means not thinking at all, then don't think at all. Don't think of anything that is a negative self-fulfilling prophecy.

When push comes to shove, the name of the game is opportunity. Opportunity can mean a lot of things. Opportunity can be found anywhere and in anything. What is an opportunity? An opportunity is that space in life available to your creative manifestation. It doesn't matter how small that space is; it is yours. It is the opportunity to be alone for a minute, the opportunity to contemplate, or the opportunity to do or not to do. Opportunity is always there. There is always something in front of you that says, "Here it is."

Getting the Most Out of Life

This leads us into the nitty-gritty of the understanding:
- If we subscribe to life as individuality
- If we can recognize the limitations of the fear, the greed, the confusion and the dominance that are there
- If we are willing to mature, to grow up, and to say, "Now, wait a minute. The system is just the system. I have something I have got to do here."
- And if we can understand that events are there to produce all the elements that we want, then the end result is the opportunity to live.

Now we are ready to take consciousness and say, "How do we do this so that we get the most out of life?"

Consciousness, in relation to the human life span, has only one major commitment. It has the commitment to improve the quality of the experience. The job of consciousness in the human individual is to improve the quality of the individual's experience. That's it, folks. That is all and that is everything that it is. The reason I can be so adamant about fine-tuning this to only one point is the fact that consciousness is connected to the Universe. It knows that it knows. It sees the Universe in totality. That is not a job to consciousness. Consciousness is the attachment to the Universe, and everything it needs to know is there.

Consciousness is not attached to the human animal. It is attached to the Universe so there is nothing for it to do. Its main job is to improve the quality of the experience because that, in your human form, will add to over-all knowledge of consciousness at this level.

- What does consciousness know? *It knows everything that it has gone through.*
- What doesn't consciousness know? *What it hasn't gone through.*
- What is consciousness trying to do? *It is saying, "I know that I need to know and because I find myself at this point in life (speaking on a manifested planet inside a physical vehicle) there are things about this planet and this physical vehicle that I need to know. If we are going to do it, let's do it in quality."*

Consciousness only knows quality. The human vehicle doesn't know quality. That is why we live in a low quality way. The human vehicle is an animal. It knows survival in any way it can. There is no etheric quality about the human vehicle as it exists in itself. It is a high form of animal. When consciousness is put inside a physical body, consciousness says, "No, we don't do things this way. We are not going to take the forty percent off sweater and walk around and think it is cashmere. It isn't. We are going to get quality out of life" That is the purpose of consciousness. The whole reasoning of metaphysics is to never leave the basics and always take yourself back to the basics.

<u>Basics:</u> When you are engaged in an activity and learning, and I come by and say, "How do you do that?" And you say, "Oh, it's easy. You put this to this to this." What you are telling me is knowledge. You are telling me how something works, and you are giving me the steps. That's knowledge. Now, I come by at another time and ask, "How do you know how to do that?" And you say, "I don't know. I just know how to do it. I can't say how I know. I just know." That's wisdom. That's essence.

The difference is that consciousness is filled with wisdom of its experiences prior to this one. It has no knowledge except what is taking place at this very moment. What consciousness is doing with the physical vehicle is trying to improve the quality of the experience during the knowledge-gathering phase, which will eventually become wisdom. That is what consciousness does. If you ask if consciousness if it knows everything, the answer is yes. Consciousness knows what it knows. It doesn't know <u>how</u> it knows. It just needs to remember that it knows. It is gaining a whole new level of experience for the purpose of adding a whole new level of wisdom further down the road. That's how commitment works.

Investments

We invest in the experience so that we can deal with the knowledge that it gives us. The knowledge from that experience can be added to our level of wisdom. That is what the Universe is all about. I go back to my original statement: The reason for consciousness, at this point, is to improve the quality of the experience so that consciousness can build upon the quality of wisdom as it progresses.

That is why consciousness looks at the physical vehicle and says, "Come on! Let's get something better out of this." The physical vehicle says, "Leave me alone. All I am interested in is survival." They don't get along with each other. They fight all the time over this. The only thing that changes that is what we call 'will'. Will is the essence that is within you that makes choices to accept the good or the bad.

Consciousness really only knows a perfect solution. If I were to give consciousness two or more options, it never really has to go through any analytical motion. With those two positions, consciousness can immediately find mid-point, which is the perfect point because consciousness always knows the perfect solution. Always! However, the trick is making sure we have two points to observe. That is what this work we are doing is all about. Obviously, consciousness can't determine a mid-point if it doesn't have two points to look at. There isn't a mid-point with just one end.

To overwork consciousness is a futile exercise because you don't have to direct consciousness to the proper answer. It automatically knows the proper answer. It automatically goes to the proper solution, which, in a material sense, produces the experience to understand and learn. Eventually what you learn is added to your wisdom. Therefore, consciousness must have a polarity to deal with. It must have a plus-minus. Consciousness must have an upper level and a lower level. Without that, it cannot work.

In any event that has an upper and lower polarity, the limit is only good for the moment we see it. For example, I enter a social event and I see this gorgeous creature on the opposite side of the room. I say to myself, "Boy, that's terrific!" What I have done is set up a polarity. At that moment the polarity consciousness is strong, and it is working in the proper center mode to conclude that communication of contact. Just as I start over to her, she starts picking her nose. Here we go folks! What happened is that at the first moment of entry, I had a proper equation and then something happened within seconds that changed it. All of a sudden, I don't have the same equation anymore. I know this is an exaggerated case, but I use it to show you that this business of finding a center point can sometimes only exist in a matter of seconds and can change right in front of your eyes.

How quickly can you change when someone says something to you that you don't like? How long did it take him to say it? One word or one statement and, all of a sudden, you go from calm and easy to ready to go for the throat. That is how quick it is. The point I am trying to make is the idea of polarities. Consciousness uses polarities to find its center point in that moment only, and that moment may be very, very short.

Sometimes you are going to have to work very quickly or not at all. A lot of times you are just going to have to bail out and realize you can't handle this because you are not going in the right direction. Events have changed, and the change may not have anything to do with what you are doing. I certainly didn't make her pick her nose. That was something within her make-up that immediately made me change my intent. That kind of thing happens all the time.

There is adaptability that is inherent in the process. You have to recognize that you can't always see this thing through the way you want. Most of the time you can, but you need to realize not all the time and not every minute. Sometimes this means you make a quick change or drop it altogether. That kind of flexibility is very important in getting through your experiences.

What's the Point?

The last element we need to consider with consciousness is that when consciousness knows its center point, the body (bless its little soul) will automatically accept the decision of the consciousness. If you learn how to do this, you eliminate the worst thing you have in life, which is conflict between consciousness and the human vehicle. It doesn't matter how you look at it, the human vehicle is a natural animal in the jungle. It doesn't concern itself with any kind of refinement. There is nothing wrong with it just doing what it has to do to exist. That is the way the planet is run.

Look at any animal that is not domesticated. It lives to survive, whether that is pulling fleas and ticks off of each other, or whether that is just simply going out and bringing down a lesser animal. That is all it knows, and that is all it has to know. Humanly, that is all we are. That's okay. I don't see anything wrong with that because that is the way this planet is made. However, when consciousness is introduced, we have a different set of values. Until consciousness can work for us establishing those values, the body will always revert to its lower basic form.

I am appalled at how disinterested people have become in themselves in an animalistic sense by the way they move through life with no sense of quality. You can see it. This includes everything from unwashed bodies (which I cannot conceive of in this day and age) to just the way they present themselves in public. It's not irrational. They are just being their good animal selves, but it shows that consciousness is not used at all, or it is being used so little that it is making no effect on the individual. You have to go back to the basics: <u>What consciousness knows, the body will accept</u>. Consciousness and awareness improve the physical condition. Now we have closed the circle. Show me a person of quality and I don't care what they are, or if they have never even heard the word 'metaphysics', they are using their consciousness. They don't have to know the vocabulary.

Habit Training

Rather than bouncing around off the trees as it were, let's try to bring ourselves to some awareness of this system of consciousness determining its higher and lower levels.

That way consciousness can immediately find its center point and communicate that instantaneously to the body. The body says, "Okay, I will go along with that" so that *you* are the person of quality for *you*. That does not make it my quality, nor does it make my quality yours because it is *your* consciousness working with *your* body.

You see, what is so important about this is that consciousness does not take into consideration anything in the materialistic viewpoint. Consciousness doesn't look at a price tag and say, "This pair of shoes is $49.50, and this pair of shoes is $39.50. What can I afford?" Consciousness doesn't know that. It can afford anything it wants. It doesn't look at comparative values. It has only its own value, but its own value is predicated upon where it is within its higher and lower limits. That is the simple system applied to this material plane.

When you are finished with this thought process, you can go out to any store and take two comparative things regardless of color, size, or shape. One has a price tag of $50.00 and another $150.00, and you will know immediately which will work for you. This is not necessarily which one of *those* will work, but what will work for you. It may be one of those. Consciousness will know exactly what your center point is for that quality. Consciousness is trying to manifest through experience in the most positive way for your own benefit. It's possible that might be neither one, and you turn and walk away. Then turn and walk away! Make sure you don't complicate this with things that do not need to be there such as over-thinking.

Everything that works in the Universe works simply. We are not dealing with your mind here. We are dealing with your consciousness. That is not something that you can get a hold on viably because consciousness really permeates all the cells in your body. There isn't one little nice spot that sits in the back of your head. What appears in some sense to be your mind is not. It is your consciousness. The key to knowing one from the other is to look at high and low points when considering something. We are trying to get consciousness to look at highest point and lowest point in order to recognize mid-point. Then consciousness will tell the body, "I am at mid-point." To understand this, do not establish any price tag in your head. You let your consciousness ring the *bell*. When consciousness tells the body that it is at mid-point, your response is *"ah ha!"* This is a training habit you have to practice. It's worth the practice.

Here is an exercise for you to practice using consciousness:
1. Consider the letters of the alphabet, and tell your consciousness to go to its lowest point. That may not be the letter A.

2. Then tell your consciousness to direct your thought to the highest point in the alphabet. That may not be the letter Z. <u>You must go through these first two steps.</u>

3. Next, allow your consciousness to find some in-between point by leaving it alone. Relax. When consciousness connects to that mid-point, **you will see, in your mind's eye, a letter.**

Consciousness sees more at its highest point than you do. This is true whether we are talking dollars or marbles. It always sees more. What you need to be physically willing to consider, at this point, is far less than what consciousness sees. It always looks beyond where the physical is looking because it always has a higher value.

Here is another exercise to use as an important tool when you are under stress:

1. Immediately switch your mind off of the event. Tell your consciousness that you want your fastest breathing and your slowest breathing.

2. Breathe very fast *without hyperventilating*, then breathe very slowly and deliberately. Let consciousness find a breathing mid-point and, if you can stay there, you will harmonize. All that tension will go away immediately. This is one reason why people under tension take deep breaths. They are trying to find that mid-point, as well as, to oxygenate their system. If you make this a habit, you will find your breathing tempo changes. You will also notice changes in your respiratory rate.

You can now use these exercises of consciousness to answer the ten following questions used at the beginning of this lecture. **Do not pick up your original answers at this point**. Take a blank piece of paper, number one to ten, and write down your answers very quickly by letting consciousness answer these questions, rather than your mind that answered the questions the first time. This is not your mind operating. What is happening is that your cells are cooperating. It's as if your whole body is going down and up. The closer you can come to that feeling, the more accurate you are going to be. See if there are any changes.

Here you go:

1. I will reach my most important life goal in _____ (number of) years.

2. When my net income reaches _____ dollars, I will be wealthy.

3. The perfect partner for me is _____ years old, _____ feet tall, weighs _____, and is in _____ career.

4. The food my body could best exist on, if it were the only food available is _____.

5. The place on the planet where I would be most happy is _____.

6. I would be most satisfied with _____ number of friends.

7. The ideal number of hours for me to work each day is _____.

8. I would pay _____ dollars for a diamond ring.

9. My ideal color is _____.

10. If I could attain to any public office, it would be _____.

Now, compare your answers of what is, hopefully, consciousness at mid-point to those answers for the same ten questions your mind answered at the beginning of this lecture.

Down to Earth

What is the whole job of consciousness? Consciousness is trying to find an ideal position so that the quality of the event (or the experience) is enjoyed and absorbed as learning. That takes us back to the basics of how this works.

You must get out of the mind and not think.* It doesn't take very long. If you have to work on it, you won't get an answer. You are pushing too hard. Define the high position and low position as identity factors. Let consciousness take control within the context of the event by allowing it to drop to its lowest point and rise to its highest point. Almost immediately consciousness finds its mid-point.

In metaphysics, we call that an answer.

---

* See First Encounter Series: No. 3, *Earth and Second Earth*.

Appendix

- A <u>tree</u> indicates your anchoring and protective capabilities. It is the mother and father quality you express in the world.

- A <u>plant</u> indicates your whole body, physical expression. It is what your body manifests and exudes.

- A <u>flower</u> indicates how you express your beauty to others.

- A <u>bird</u> indicates how words leave you and are transmitted into the atmosphere. Birds chirp downwind in order for the wind to carry their song.

- A <u>fish</u> indicates your flexibility and fluidity. It is also your relationship to water on the planet.

- An <u>animal</u> indicates how you move with your authority in order to exist.

- A type of <u>mineral</u> indicates your core magnetic relationship to your skeletal structure (your bones). It is your relationship to the center of the earth.

From The Collected Works of Gregge Tiffen

Life in the World Hereafter: The Journey Continues

Life in the World Hereafter Journal

First Encounter Series:
  No. 1 Into the Universe: Extraterrestrial Activities
  No. 2 Down to Earth: Terrestrial Activities
  No. 3 Earth and Second Earth

Questions and More Questions

2010 Booklet of the Month Series:
  The Journey Continues

2009 Booklet of the Month Series:
  The Language of a Mystic

2008 Booklet of the Month Series:
  Lessons in Living

2007 Booklet of the Month Series:
  Seasonal Reflections

2006 Thanksgiving: The Power of Prayer
2006 Winter Solstice: The Christmas Story

All publications are available
directly from P Systems
P.O. Box 12754
La Jolla, CA 92039

For Credit card orders and detailed descriptions visit:
www.P-SystemsInc.com/publications
For bulk orders call toll free: 1.888.658.0668

www.ingramcontent.com/pod-product-compliance
Lightning Source LLC
LaVergne TN
LVHW011729060526
838200LV00051B/3093